Preface

The foundation of our free enterprise system is entrepreneurship. After a rather lengthy period of decline, the entrepreneurial spirit is enjoying an incredible revival in the United States. Indeed, the entrepreneur may well come to characterize American business in the 1980s and beyond in much the same way that the organization man characterized business in the 1950s. Books on entrepreneurship are being published in increasing numbers, and some 130 leading universities are teaching courses, providing majors, and even offering degrees in entrepreneurship.[1]

The key ingredient in making a successful entrepreneur is the ability to plan, and preparing a formal business plan is crucial to the ultimate success of an enterprise. The business plan is important for a number of reasons. Initially, it evaluates the viability of the venture. Then it assists the entrepreneur in establishing his goals and objectives. Next, it guides the entrepreneur in selecting the proper methods for achieving his goals and objectives in a timely fashion. Finally, it is the principal vehicle for the entrepreneur to obtain start-up venture capital or money for the expansion of his on-going business if outside capital is required.

There are numerous volumes in print on planning and the planning process, but these are typically written for use by the long established, large corporations.[2] There are also a number of books which have

---

[1] See Vesper, Karl H. *Entrepreneurship Education: A Bicentennial Compendium,* Milwaukee: Center for Venture Management, 1976.

[2] See, for example, Welsch, Glenn A. *Budgeting: Profit Planning and Control,* Fourth Ed. Englewood Cliffs, NJ: Prentice-Hall, Inc., 1976.

recently appeared on new venture creation and small business management, but developing a business plan is the subject of only a small fraction of the contents of these works.[3] In the course on Entrepreneurship and the New Enterprise offered at the Jesse H. Jones Graduate School of Administration of Rice University, the authors have drawn upon a number of source materials to illustrate how to develop a business plan. A similar approach has been employed in the Jones Graduate School Executive Development seminar on "How to Develop a Business Plan." The combined experience of presenting these courses and seminars over the past several years, together with the perceived need of having a single volume devoted exclusively to writing a business plan, caused the authors to prepare the present volume.

Business Planning for the Entrepreneur is intended to fill a gap in the growing literature on entrepreneurship. College and university students taking courses in entrepreneurship should find this book to be a valuable learning aid. Practitioners starting their first new business will be shown, in detail, precisely how to write a business plan in order to enhance the chances for the success of the new entity and to assist in raising capital. Every budding entrepreneur needs to have a short, concise treatment on how to prepare a business plan, and the authors believe this book provides valuable insights on the methodology of planning and the mechanics of plan preparation. The principles apply equally to small and large ventures, and entrepreneurs who have established businesses will also benefit from the book. Several examples of actual plans that the authors and others have written are included in appendices at the end of the book.

Edward E. Williams
Salvatore E. Manzo

---

[3] See, for example, Mancuso, J. R. *How to Start, Finance, and Manage Your Own Small Business.* Englewood Cliffs, NJ: Prentice-Hall, Inc., 1978.

Business Planning for the Entrepreneur

How to Write and Execute a Business Plan

Edward E. Williams

Henry Gardiner Symonds Professor
Jesse H. Jones Graduate School of Administration
Rice University

and

Salvatore E. Manzo

Director of Executive Development
Jesse H. Jones Graduate School of Administration
Rice University

 VAN NOSTRAND REINHOLD COMPANY

80467

Library of Congress Catalog Card Number: 82-8658
ISBN: 0-442-28970-7

Manufactured in the United States of America

Published by Van Nostrand Reinhold Company Inc.
135 West 50th Street
New York, New York 10020

Van Nostrand Reinhold Company Limited
Molly Millars Lane
Wokingham, Berkshire RG11 2PY, England

Van Nostrand Reinhold
480 Latrobe Street
Melbourne, Victoria 3000, Australia

Macmillan of Canada
Division of Gage Publishing Limited
164 Commander Boulevard
Agincourt, Ontario M1S 3C7, Canada

15 14 13 12 11 10 9 8 7 6 5 4 3 2

Library of Congress Cataloging in Publication Data

Williams, Edward E.
    Business planning for the entrepreneur.

    Includes bibliographies and index.
    1. Planning.   3. Entrepreneur.   I. Manzo,
Slavatore E.   II. Title.
HD30.28.W54   1982   658.4'012   82-8658
ISBN 0-442-28970-7   AACR2

Acknowledgments

The authors wish to acknowledge the contribution of the excellent business plan on Electric Cars of Houston, contained in the appendix, which was prepared by Braintrust Incorporated, a Houston management services firm. They also acknowledge and thank the administrative staff of the Jesse H. Jones Graduate School of Administration, Rice University, for their excellent support in the preparation of the manuscript.

Contents

1
An Overview of the Planning Process

A person who wishes to form a new enterprise must know *what* sort of business will prosper and *why* it will become successful. He must also know *where* he wants his business to go, *how* he expects to get it there, *when* he anticipates reaching the goals he has established for his venture, and *who* will be responsible for carrying out the plan. The strategies associated with determining the what, why, where, how, when, and who of a new venture are spelled out in a *business plan.*

The business plan is written for two audiences. The *complete business plan* is prepared by the entrepreneur to guide him through the perilous stages of founding a new business. The *summary (or financing) business plan* is used as a vehicle to raise money for the fledgling endeavor. The organizational structure of both requires some familiarity with planning procedures and processes. This chapter is intended to provide that familiarity.

PLANNING FOR THE NEW OR THE SEASONED ENTERPRISE

A business plan is an important success ingredient for the new business and the existing one. For many firms, planning only begins *after* the firm has advanced beyond the infant stage. This is a serious mistake. Planning is needed *at all stages* of business development from inception to maturity. Starting a business without a plan is like beginning an extended automobile journey without a road map. Unless the route is well known, the driver is very likely to lose time or get lost. Of course, there are businesses that are so familiar to the experienced entrepreneur that a detailed plan may be unnecessary.

Nevertheless, regardless of how experienced one may be, a plan of some kind is essential to success. This is especially so for those entrepreneurial ventures that are new, unique, or complex, and for which early success and rapid growth are most likely. Such endeavors cannot be approached in a "seat-of-the-pants" or "gut-reaction" manner. Planning is the process by which things are made to happen in an orderly, timely, and progressive manner. The business plan is essential to the success of new or seasoned businesses, whether small or large.

WHAT IS PLANNING ALL ABOUT?

Planning is the process which permits an entity to become what it wishes to become. It is the identification of opportunities and the allocation of the requisite resources to exploit those opportunities. It is the rational determination of where you are now, where you want to be, and how you should go about getting there. Planning is a necessary ingredient in the successful management of your personal life as well as your business life. Most people wander down their personal lives with no clear-cut mission in mind. They really do not know from one day to the next what they want to accomplish, and for this reason they usually accomplish very little. The successful individual, on the other hand, usually knows what he wishes to accomplish and has a definite strategy for achieving his objectives. A prominent Houston entrepreneur, who founded what is now the largest waste disposal firm in the world, carries around index cards in his pocket with his goals for the particular month and what he has done to achieve those goals.[1] He is very meticulous about this procedure. He is also a very disciplined person and this is why he was able to build a $600 million corporation from one small garbage truck.

Most people fail not because they lack intelligence or talent. They fail because they have no clear sense of what they want to achieve. Similarly, most new businesses fail not because the founder is stupid or lazy or insufficiently capitalized. They fail because the *business concept* was improperly developed and because a detailed plan for

---

[1] See Fatjo, Tom J. Jr., and Miller, Keith. *With No Fear of Failure.* Waco, TX: Word Books, 1981.

success was not worked out in advance. Of course, many new business ideas are simply bad ideas. There is little chance that the fiftieth imitation of an already successful business in a defined area is going to be sufficiently different to justify the time, money, and effort required to make a go of it. However, a well thought-out business plan would probably have concluded that the chance of success was minimal and would thus have saved the entrepreneur from ultimate failure.

Why Plan?

Planning is carried out to determine what must be done this week, or this month, or this year so that the enterprise will be in the desired position next month, or next year, or even five years hence. It is not concerned with future decisions but with the future effect of present decisions. Planning is not something you do today for today's benefit. Rather, it is something you do now for the benefit of the enterprise down the road. Planning jumps ahead to the end of the time period under consideration and works back to determine what must be done at what intervals in time to maximize the chances that the objectives of the entity will be attained.

Planning may be considered in its proper context by analyzing just what the business enterprise does. In essence, the enterprise is a social entity that puts together people, capital, and materials to produce products and services (see Figure 1-1). This is what business is all about. Of course, the process of putting people, capital, and materials together generates costs while the sale of the ensuing products and services produces revenues. Profits are the difference between revenues and costs and typically figure into the objectives of the enterprise. It is the calculated manipulation of both the outputs (revenues) and the inputs (costs) to generate profits that requires planning.

To be sure, not every profitable business was planned that way. Some companies, like some people, are successful by sheer accident. It just happens. Most failures, however, are not planned. They also "just happen." Take the case of a typical would-be entrepreneur who decides to go into the restaurant business. He buys the equipment a restaurant equipment salesman says he needs (maybe putting in $50,000 to $100,000 of his life's savings), finds a location, hires a

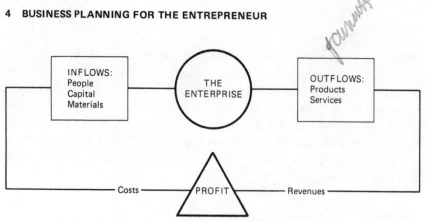

Figure 1-1. The Business Enterprise.

cook and a few waiters, and annouces to the world: "I'm in business." The doors open. Business the first day is slow. It picks up a little after a couple of months. Three months later, the entrepreneur is looking for "additional working capital" to keep the business afloat. If he finds it, he may be in business for a few more months. Eventually, however, the business runs out of cash and fails. Why? In the first place, the entrepreneur did not plan the _economics_ of the business. Was it a viable idea in the first place? How did his restaurant differ from the 500 other restaurants in the city? Why would anyone wish to patronize this particular restaurant? Second, the entrepreneur did not plan a _marketing strategy._ How were customers to be attracted? How were they to find out about the existence of the new restaurant? What prices would be compatible with the clientele envisaged for the business and the type of food offered? Third, the entrepreneur did not have a _production_ and _personnel plan._ How many employees would be required? Did the fact that he hired four waiters and never had enough business but for two have something to do with the ultimate failure? How was food to be prepared? How was it to be served? Finally, the entrepreneur did not have a _financial plan._ How much money was really required to buy equipment? Was the outright purchase of equipment the best policy or would a leasing arrangement have made more sense? How much working capital was necessary to see the business through the early unprofitable months? How long should it have taken before the break-even point was reached? What contingency plans did the entrepreneur have in the event the firm did not break even as quickly as anticipated? How much profit could the firm ultimately make? Given the required investment, was the expected return on that investment sufficient to justify putting the funds into this particular business?

All of the above questions should be addressed in a properly developed business plan. Of course, the average entrepreneur has a vague answer to most of them before he starts business, but rarely can the stark realities, the possible inconsistencies of assumptions, and the action path required to assure success be known unless a *written document* is carefully prepared *before* the doors are opened and the first dollar is invested. It is for these reasons that bankers and venture capitalists *insist* on a written plan before they put any of their money in a new (or existing) business. The entrepreneur owes it to himself to be just as careful about how he invests his money and, perhaps more importantly, his time. To answer the question: Why plan? If you do not, the risk of failure is greatly increased.

Advantages of Planning

The major advantage of planning, of course, is that success usually requires it. There are a number of other reasons a new (or existing) business should plan, however. Among the other advantages of planning are the following:

1. *Planning forces an early consideration of essential goals and basic policies.* A surprising number of businesses are established without a clear-cut mission in mind. Why was the firm formed? What is its purpose? What are the goals of the enterprise? Which policies are best calculated to achieve these goals? Planning makes it necessary to answer these questions and therefore helps the entrepreneur focus on the raison d'être for the business.

2. *Planning requires a sound organizational structure.* In order to implement a planning system, people who will accomplish certain tasks at specific times must be identified. If a firm lacks an adequate organizational structure, it will become obvious that the tasks cannot be performed. Thus, planning calls attention to the personnel requirements of the enterprise in advance of need and assists the entrepreneur in establishing a proper organization even though it probably will be simple and small to begin with.

3. *Planning compels participation.* Businesses do not plan. People do. For an entity to achieve the objectives it has established, it takes the collective efforts and cooperation of all the members of the organization. Successful planning necessitates the participation of all individuals who are affected by the plan and, therefore, stimulates a participatory environment. This is particularly useful for the company that is still in its infancy. At this stage, most enterprises are very much under the total direction of the founding entrepreneur, and anything which assists in getting the involvement of others in the organization is useful.

4. *Planning promotes motivation and good human relations.* This is a corollary to the previous advantage. Most entrepreneurs are not people oriented. Usually, they are "thing" or "idea" oriented. Often they forget that it takes people to make an enterprise successful. The planning process, by focusing attention on the roles that human beings must play in the company, engenders a better understanding on the part of the entrepreneur of the importance of people and thus indirectly contributes to better human relations in the firm. By the same token, when the appropriate elements of a plan are disseminated to the employees for a clearer understanding of their roles in the success of the venture, they will be better motivated to be productive.

5. *Planning necessitates quantification.* A good plan is both a narrative and a quantitative statement. Objectives are spelled out numerically, and quantitative standards are thus specified from which success (or lack thereof) can be measured. Planning causes the entrepreneur to state in hard numbers what he wants to accomplish, what environment he expects to operate in, and what results are hoped for. Planning thus eliminates some of the fuzziness that often accompanies establishing a new enterprise.

6. *Planning focuses management attention on relevent factors.* What are the key variables that will determine whether or not the enterprise is a success? What values are these variables expected to assume over the next few months (years)? Is the level of overall economic activity (Gross National Product) important? How about the level of interest rates? Is the rate of inflation a factor? What about demographic factors? Planning requires the entrepreneur to think about these external variables that may be crucial to the success of the firm. What about the price of the product produced

by the entrepreneur? Can he set that price, or must the prices of competitors also be considered? How important will an advertising program be? What about production costs? People costs? How much money has to be raised? Is it critical if enough money cannot be found immediately? These internal variables must also be determined and quantified.

7. *Planning contributes to management by exception.* Since planning focuses attention on the relevant factors determing the success of the enterprise, it also allows the entrepreneur (and others in management) to known when variables take on unusual or unexpected values. So long as expected results are occurring, there is no need for management to waste time considering them. It is only when an exceptional value occurs that managers should be concerned. When unexpected values happen it may be necessary to employ the *control* function of management (i.e., the feedback mechanism designed to assure that actual results conform to planned ones), or to change the plan. It may happen that exogenous variables outside the control of the firm have made it impossible to achieve the results originally desired. Thus, it may be necessary to replan and set forth more realistic objectives in light of the impact of the external environment.

8. *Planning forces feedback of information and periodic reappraisal.* In order to assess whether or not planned variables have taken on expected or unexpected values, there must be continuous feedback of information as well as a periodic reappraisal of all internal and external variables and their impact on the enterprise. This means that the entrepreneur must be continually aware of progress and problems in all the important elements that determine the success of the business. Periodic reappraisal requires the systematic feedback of information and involves both the control function of management and the replanning function.

9. *Planning is consistent with management by objectives.* It has become increasingly recognized by management experts that management by objectives (MBO) is the most scientific method for an enterprise to be conducted. MBO is scientific in that the goals and objectives of the firm are established and then requisite patterns of behavior *follow logically* from them. Certain events must occur for the goals and objectives to be achieved, and the task of management is to see that these events do, in fact, occur.

SUMMARY AND CONCLUSIONS

Planning is an essential first step in any human endeavor of consequence, whether at the highest levels of government or for the smallest business enterprise. The planning process requires that your goals and objectives be defined and quantified, the resources necessary to achieve established goals and objectives be specified, the external and internal forces which affect success be identified and evaluated, and the steps and timing required to accomplish desired results be enumerated. A good plan will help the entrepreneur to be realistic in his judgment while helping him make logical decisions.

In an era of economic difficulty, where the influences of external forces on businesses are increasingly important, "seat-of-the-pants" management is a thing of the past. In order to minimize risk exposure and to increase the opportunity for success, the entrepreneur must engage in a systematic and methodical planning process, and he must see to it that the plan initially formulated is kept current when assumptions or conditions change.

It is also essential to realize that the plan is a management tool and represents the beginning of the entrepreneurial venture. The results achieved will only be as good as the quality of the plan's execution and its subsequent periodic updating based upon those results. A sound business plan is one which provides the direction necessary to be successful, yet maintains a flexibility to take advantage of new opportunities or to permit adjustments when assumptions or conditions change.

KEY TERMS

Enterprise. A social entity that puts together people, capital, and materials to produce products and/or services.

Planning. The process which permits an entity to become what it wishes to become. The identification of opportunities and the allocation of the requisite resources to exploit those opportunities. The rational determination of where you are now, where you want to be, and how you should go about getting there.

REFERENCES

Ackoff, Russell L. *A Concept of Corporate Planning.* New York: J. Wiley & Sons, Inc., 1972.

Ansoff, H. I., Declerck, R. P., and Hayes, R. L. *From Strategic Planning to Strategic Management.* New York: J. Wiley & Sons, Inc., 1976.

Christopher, William F. *The Achieving Enterprise.* New York: American Management Association, 1974.

Ewing, David. *The Human Side of Planning.* New York: Macmillan Company, 1969.

Fatjo, Tom J., Jr., and Miller, Keith. *With No Fear of Failure.* Waco, TX: Word Books, 1981.

Gup, Benton E. *Guide to Strategic Planning.* New York: McGraw-Hill Book Company, 1980.

Hussey, David. *Corporate Planning.* Oxford, England: Pergamon Press, 1974.

——. *Introducing Corporate Planning.* Oxford, England: Pergamon Press, 1971.

Jankowski, Patrick. "Cashing In On Your Business Plan." *Houston,* September, 1981, pp. 22–25.

Mancuso, Joseph R. *How to Start, Finance, and Manage Your Own Small Business.* Englewood Cliffs, NJ: Prentice-Hall, Inc., 1978.

Mockler, Robert J. *Business Planning and Policy Formation.* New York: Appleton-Century-Crofts, Inc., 1972.

Osgood, William R. *Basics of Successful Business Planning.* New York: AMACOM, a division of American Management Associations, 1980.

Schoennauer, Alfred W. *The Formulation and Implementation of Corporate Objectives and Strategies.* Oxford, OH: Planning Executives Institute, 1972.

Steiner, George A. *Top Management Planning.* New York: Macmillan Company, 1969.

Taylor, Bernard, and Sparkes, John R. *Corporate Strategy and Planning.* New York: Halsted Press, 1977.

Vesper, Karl H. *Entrepreneurship Education: A Bicentennial Compendium.* Milwaukee: Center for Venture Management, 1976.

——. *New Venture Strategies.* Englewood Cliffs, NJ: Prentice-Hall, Inc., 1980.

Welsch, Glenn A. *Budgeting: Profit Planning and Control.* Fourth Ed. Englewood Cliffs, NJ: Prentice-Hall, 1976.

2
Planning and the Entrepreneurial Function

A *business plan* is a written document describing the what, why, where, how, when, and who of developing and operating a new (or existing) venture. It is particularly useful to the entrepreneur because it forces him to come to grips immediately with the basic policies of his business. He must consider why he is establishing a new business or continuing to operate a given one (goals) and what specifically he hopes to accomplish (objectives). He must contemplate what resources will be required to reach the goals and achieve the objectives that have been set.

The *complete business plan* is an entire planning document that includes an introduction, a summary of the key characteristics of the industry and proposed (existing) venture, *pro forma* financial statements, a complete analysis of the industry, the form and organizational structure of the venture, a strategic plan, an operating plan, and appendices including pertinent contracts, technical information, and support data. The complete plan requires the entrepreneur to quantify in hard numbers what is expected to be done and is thus a vital management tool for enhancing the chances for success of the new (or existing) enterprise. The *summary business plan* (or *financing plan*) contains parts of the complete plan which venture capitalists, bankers, and other financiers might wish to review prior to committing funds to the enterprise. It should include all elements of the complete plan except the strategic plan (to be discussed later), the operating plan (to be discussed later), and certain appendices. Thus, the complete business plan and the summary (financing) plan are prepared to provide the entrepreneur and his financial backers with benchmarks which can be used to measure the relative success of the new business. Quantification of planned results instills at all levels of management the timely, careful, and adequate consideration of all the relevant factors that go into decision making.

PLANNING AND GOOD BUSINESS MANAGEMENT

Before an entrepreneur can fruitfully plan he must consider what he believes the real role of management to be. There are two conceptual extremes that can be delineated. The first is referred to as the *market theory* which views the role of management as reacting to events as they occur (crisis management).[1] The opposite is the *planning and control theory* which considers the managerial role as being comprised of decisions and actions today that are forward-looking and which are based upon assessments of future expected developments. This concept rests upon the belief that the primary success factor in an enterprise is the competence of management to plan and control the activities of the business.

Management Functions

In planning for and controlling the variables that significantly affect the success of an enterprise, management must continually: (1) plan, (2) organize, (3) staff, (4) direct, and (5) control.[2] These five responsibilities or functions are depicted in Figure 2-1. Most firms that have "good management" are those which have adopted management styles responding to the need for imaginative use of these five basic management functions. You should, however, be sensitive to

[1] During periods of increasing uncertainty, there is a tendency for business (and other) organizations to reject planning concepts and revert to crisis management. The hyperinflation and other economic difficulties experienced throughout the world over the past few years have caused some managers, unfortunately, to regress to older, seat-of-the-pants strategies. See Ekman, Jan. "The Scrapping of the Forecasts," *Euromoney,* Oct., 1981, pp. 222–229.

[2] These functions are identified by Koontz, Harold, and O'Donnell, Cyril. *Principles of Management, An Analysis of Managerial Functions,* Fifth Ed. New York: McGraw-Hill Book Co., Inc., 1972.

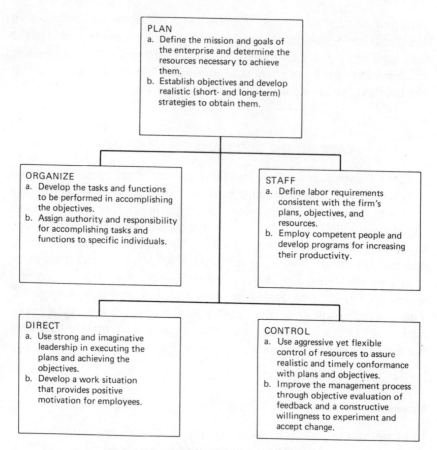

Figure 2-1. The Functions of Management.

the fact that a very real hazard exists in overformalizing the management process. In any situation, inflexible administration will hurt the ability of an enterprise to respond to changing circumstances.

A fact that the entrepreneur should always be aware of is that the motivation of human resources is central to effective management and success in any enterprise. He must understand that the participation of employees in the establishment of company goals, plans, and policies has come to be recognized as one of the more useful approaches to motivation and productivity improvement at all organizational levels. Proper planning provides a method for resolving problems associated with conflicting goals since participation by all levels of management is required in the development of goals and related policies and their implementation. Thus, planning is a mental attitude as well as a useful managerial tool.

Accounting and Management Information Systems

Although planning is related to accounting, it is not an accounting procedure but rather a management technique. The accounting system becomes involved in planning in the following ways:

1. Accounting provides inputs of historical data that are relevant for analytical purposes in the development of the business plan.
2. The financial phase of a profit plan is structured in an accounting format.
3. Actual data utilized in the measurement of performance is provided by the accounting system.

As a company grows, it develops the need to be able to coordinate information in order to evaluate progress in execution of the plan and to anticipate changes in market and profit situations. The purpose, of course, is to prevent the development of an unprofitable situation and the entrepreneur may wish to incorporate a management information system (MIS) into the planning process. An MIS should be designed to assist in predicting, in comparing actual results with predictions, and reducing deviations between predictions and actual results. A typical MIS flow chart is depicted in Figure 2-2. As can be seen, historical data are reduced to meaningful summaries. These summaries are then analyzed by management to produce predictions which are then used to prepare *pro forma* statements that are consistent with the objectives of the entity. Once actual operating results are known, these may be used to ascertain if the deviations between actual and *pro forma* results were caused by poor implementation of the selected strategy or whether the predictions or budgets require revision (replanning).

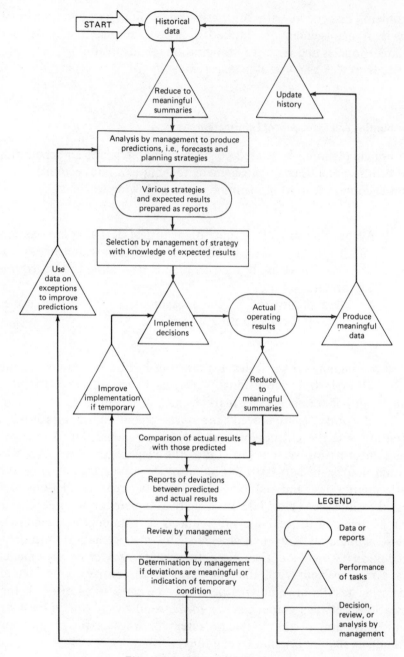

Figure 2-2. MIS and Planning.

Who Plans?

Who plans in an organization? For many entrepreneurs, especially if they are still running a "one-person show," every position in the firm from chairman down to worker is filled by the entrepreneur. This does not mean that planning is unimportant to the small organization. What it does mean is that the entrepreneur may simply have to spend a great deal of his time implementing and will have less time for planning. When he is serving in the role of chairman or president, however, he should spend much of his time planning (see Figure 2-3).

When a business is first established, it is frequently the case that the entrepreneur has so many things to do that he does not have time to think about where he is and where he is going. He has too many operating details to take care of. Sometimes there is little that he can do about this situation. This means that the entrepreneur has to put in another hour or two a day to make sure the other eighteen or nineteen are productive. That one hour of planning during the day will result in saving sufficient time out of the rest to justify its investment.

As the firm begins to grow, the entrepreneur needs to spend more and more time evaluating progress and thinking about the future position of the enterprise. What new ideas are available to reduce the cost of operation, to expand into new areas, to make the company

Position	Proportion of Time Spent Planning
Chairman	90–100
President	80–90
Executive Vice President	70–80
Vice President	50–70
Division Head	30–50
Department Head	10–30
Assistant Department Head	5–20
Supervisor	5–10
Clerical Staff	0–5
Worker	0–5

Figure 2-3. Who Plans in an Organization?

more profitable? It might be rewarding for each entrepreneur to keep a diary of his activities during a particular week and compare them to the proportions shown in Figure 2-3. You can easily see how much planning effort is required to keep an organization operating effectively, and it is alarmingly easy to put off the more loosely defined job of planning in favor of managing daily activities. The entrepreneur must, however, avoid this temptation if he is to serve his proper role: that of directing the enterprise towards its goals while assuring long-term survival.

The control and feedback functions are devoted to making sure that planned events happen. Employees who govern whether planned events are to occur spend most of their time implementing and controlling. Nevertheless, every employee plans to some extent, and everyone in the business should be involved in the planning process in some manner. If the entrepreneur does not get others involved, his planning may become a one-person affair. If the entrepreneur plans alone and then gives the plan to the people who work for him and says, "This is what we are going to do," then progress will not be as satisfactory as it can be if the employees had some input in the planning process. Everyone has to understand where the firm is moving and why it is moving in that direction, and they must be made to feel that they had some influence on the plan. One characteristic of an effective leader is the degree to which he encourages and permits subordinates at various working and management levels to participate in the planning function.

There are two other reasons for involving all employees in the planning process: First, everyone has ideas. Sometimes, the most junior employee will come up with ideas that the president has not thought about. Unless these people are involved in the planning process, good ideas may be lost. Second, if the entrepreneur does not have everyone involved, they are simply not going to be committed to the plan; and if they are not committed to the plan, it is not going to be successful.

Of course, what has been said above does not mean that all the employees of a firm should gather around a table and plan for the next year. The chief executive officer and the key people who report to him will typically do most of the long-range planning which involves the setting of goals and objectives of the enterprise. All employees. however, should be involved in the determination of how to operate the business most effectively in the period immediately ahead.   Short-range planning should involve every manager in the organization in mapping out his part in accomplishing overall enterprise objectives.   Every employee in the firm should understand his role in making the plan successful and should be encouraged to give inputs to his immediate supervisor which may affect the objectives to be established and the means of achieving those objectives.

WHAT IS A BUSINESS PLAN?

First of all, a business plan is *not* a budget. A budget merely defines a revenue and an expense stream. Budgets result from plans. A plan is a narrative and quantitative statement depicting *what* is to be done; *why, where,* and *how* it is to be done; *when* it is to be done; and *who* is to do it.   A good plan will specifically define what business the firm is in. This may seem like a fairly simple matter, but it is often the case that many entrepreneurs have difficulty carefully articulating just exactly what they do or intend to do.   Interestingly, many entrepreneurs have gone broke because they did not define in detail what business they thought they were engaged in.   Consider the following.

A businessman on the East Coast maintained a dock and sold and rented boats.   He thought he was in the marina business, but when he got into trouble and asked for outside help, he learned that he was not just in the marina business.   In fact, he was in several businesses. He was in the restaurant business, with a dockside cafe serving meals to boating parties. He was in the real estate business, buying and selling lots. He was in the fuel service business, buying and selling gasoline and oil. He was in the repair business, buying parts and hiring mechanics. He also sold and rented boats and motors. This entrepreneur was actually involved in several totally different businesses and had difficulty deciding how much money and time to invest in the assortment of activities in which he was engaged.   Unfortunately, he had slim resources and these were fragmented.   Since he had never prepared a business plan, the entrepreneur really did not know what to expect. He did not know which lines of business would be profitable and which would not, and he really did not understand how his various activities pieced together. Ultimately, the entrepreneur prepared a business plan and defined his business as being that of buying, selling, and servicing boats and motors.   He decided he was not in the restaurant or real estate business.   Having thus decided what his essential commercial activity was, the entrepreneur could then concentrate his energies and resources on the best strategy for selling, renting, and servicing his boats and motors (a marketing plan); for buying his products, supplies and equipment and employing personnel (a production plan); and for efficiently raising and utilizing his capital (a financial plan).

Statement of Goals

Once it has been determined what business the firm is in, the plan should then advance to being more specific about what is to be accomplished during the planning period.   At this stage it becomes important for the entrepreneur to determine his overall business goals (pinpointing just why he is in business in the first place and what he wants to accomplish).   For example, an entrepreneur may have determined that he is in business for three specific reasons: (1) to make enough money to be independently wealthy by the time he reaches age 40, (2) to engage in an activity that is enjoyable and challenging, and (3) to build an organization that will provide employment and a product or service useful to the community.   Of course, it is important for the entrepreneur to be sure that he does not have inconsistent goals.   One of the purposes of the business plan is to force the entrepreneur to be specific about his reasons for being in business.   These should be written down.   The process of sorting out goals sometimes enables the entrepreneur to determine that he does have conflicting goals.   Obviously, if in the back of his mind the entrepreneur wished to build a profitable business and yet also wanted to satisfy desires that might conflict with building a profitable business, he would make inconsistent decisions and would accomplish none of his goals.   More will be said about goal specification and the process of goal realization in Chapter 3, but an outline of the process is presented in Figure 2-4.

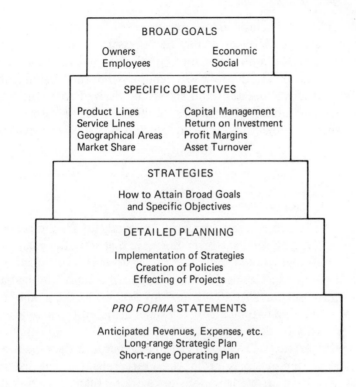

Figure 2-4. Establishing Goals and Objectives.

Establishment of Objectives

Once the goals are established, it becomes necessary to set fairly concrete quantitative objectives that are consistent with the goals. For example, the objective of increasing sales by 10% next year might be postulated together with an objective to decrease costs by 2%, to increase profits by 15%, and to improve return on investment from 14% to 16%. These percentage objectives can then be translated into dollar amounts and tested for internal consistency. Such queries as this might be made: Is it consistent to increase profits by 15% while return on investment advances by 2%?

Obviously, emanating from the general objectives will be rather more specific subobjectives that must be met in order to satisfy the principal objectives. Thus, in order to realize the sales and profit increases established, it may be necessary to add sales person-nel, to increase the number of units produced, and to make certain capital expenditures to improve efficiency. All of these subobjectives must be mutually consistent and should be derived from the overall percentage and dollar objectives. A more in-depth discussion of setting specific objectives and subobjectives will be provided in Chapter 4.

The Role of People in Setting Goals and Objectives

People considerations clearly become important in setting goals and objectives. In goal setting, for instance, is it strictly the goals of the entrepreneur that should rule the progress of the organization or should the individual goals of those people who report immediately to the entrepreneur also be taken into account? What about the goals of middle management, of the supervisors, of the people at the lowest working levels? It should be clear that all human beings have their own aspirations. The number three manager in the organization may have different goals from the entrepreneur. The assembly worker may have different reasons for working than a vice president. Hence, a realistic business plan will take into account the possibility that all members of the organization may not be pulling in the same direction. A good plan, however, will also attempt to reconcile any goal conflicts that may exist and should provide policy direction when particular employees have personal goals that are inconsistent with those of the enterprise as a whole. Needless to say, at this juncture the managerial style and the personal make-up of the entrepreneur become important. Some entrepreneurs subscribe to the so-called "golden rule" theory of management. This maxim specifies that, "He who hath the gold maketh the rules." There is nothing wrong with this philosphy, but the entrepreneur who manages in this fashion should be aware of the fact that other members of his organization may not share his goals. These goals should be spelled out carefully, however, in order to determine possible interpersonal goal conflicts. Other entrepreneurs will adopt a more participatory managerial style and will invite goal setting from other members of the organization.   Once again, the possibility of conflict still arises and planning helps identify potential conflicts.

Beyond the setting of goals and objectives, the roles of people also become important in carrying out the plan.   The question of who is to do what is crucial and one way to answer it is by having a series of company organizational and functional charts.   The first in the series is the organization as it is now.   Functional boxes should be detailed and should identify individuals assigned to those functions.   In the case of the new venture, where the entrepreneur is the only employee of the firm, it may well be the case that the entrepreneur fills eight, nine, or more boxes all by himself.   Nevertheless, it is important to specify *what these functions are* so that he can plan for future personnel needs as the company grows.   Future organization charts should also be detailed to suggest how functional arrangements may be subdivided as the organization becomes more complex.   For multiple year plans, it is a good idea to have an organization chart prepared for each planning year in which material change takes place.   More on this subject will be presented in Chapter 4.

The Role of Timing in the Planning Process

Finally, the issue of timing must be confronted in the business plan.   Timing identifies *when* certain things must be done or certain plateaus reached.   Is the objective to have a 10% increase in the sales next year, an 8% increase the year after that, a 6% increase the year after that, etc.?   Timing and time demarcation are so important in the time planning process that two very different kinds of time planning are frequently designated.

Strategic or long-range planning is the determination of what products or services the enterprise is going to make available to which class of customers in specified geographical areas.   Strategic planning takes into account the broad goals of the organization and usually deals in horizons of several years; It is not unusual for a business plan to have a four-or five-year time horizon, although for a new business this would be difficult to develop with a high confidence factor.   Some businesses, in fact, plan ten or more years in the future. To a large extent, the proper time horizon depends upon the history of the firm, whether it is old or new, and the environment in which it operates. Long planning horizons are possible for on-going businesses that are fairly stable and where the goals of the entrepreneur are reasonably ambitious. Shorter planning horizons are necessary for new businesses, for those in highly cyclic industries, and for high-risk ventures. Strategic planning is ordinarily done by a small number of people in the top of the organization using agreed upon assumptions. This does not mean that strategic planning cannot involve almost all levels in the firm. Nevertheless, strategic planning can become very unwieldy if too many people participate in the process.

Operating or short-range planning, on the other hand, is the determination of how to run the business effectively in the months immediately ahead while progress is made towards the objectives of the strategic plan. Operating planning should involve every manager in the organization and can conceivably involve every employee directly or indirectly. Typically, the operating plan is done on a one-year basis. It is the plan from which budgets are prepared and the one from which the control element derives. The operating plan will frequently be broken down into quarters and for many firms, monthly and even weekly time periods are considered, especially in the feedback of information for evaluation of progress.

THE PLANNING DOCUMENTS

The planning process culminates in the preparation of planning documents. In general, two formalized plans will be prepared (see Figure 2-5). The first, the *complete* plan, is intended for the internal use of the entrepreneur and his subordinates. In some ways, it becomes the heart of the business. It should outline the mission of the enterprise and define the business opportunity. It should provide a statement of the basic goals and specific objectives and subobjectives for the planning period under consideration. The major internal and external variables affecting the enterprise should be enumerated and assumptions should be made about the likely

The Complete Plan	The Summary (Financing) Plan
Introduction	Introduction
Summary of industry and venture	Summary of industry and venture
Pro forma financial statements	*Pro forma* financial statements
Complete industry analysis	Complete industry analysis
Form and organizational structure of company	Form and organizational structure of company
The strategic plan	Selected appendices
The operating plan	
Appendices	

Figure 2-5. The Planning Documents.

values for each important variable. A list of the strengths and weakness of the venture should be constructed with a complete analysis of each. Finally, a quantitative statement by year should be formulated which would include *pro forma* statements of revenues, expenses, and cash flow, and *pro forma* balance sheets. This quantitative statement should be the logical outcome from the narrative analysis previously done in the plan.

The complete plan will include in it both the strategic plan and the operating or short-range plan. The operating plan should be considerably more specific in nature and should provide quarterly, perhaps monthly, and conceivably weekly budget figures. Nevertheless, all parts of the complete plan should be considered tentative, even the budget numbers. Planning is a continuous process and must be kept flexible at all times. It is not something an entrepreneur does as he is founding a new business and then forgets about. Neither is it an activity that the growing enterprise engages in on an "annual basis." The firm that "sets aside" the last two weeks of the fiscal year to "plan" for the next year is simply going through an exercise. Serious planning goes on throughout the year, and plans may have to change to correspond to an ever-changing environment. If a major assumption is no longer valid, replanning may be necessary, and a new plan formulated. For this reason, the complete business plan should *never* be a bound document. It should be placed in a looseleaf notebook where pages can be substituted as required.

The second formalized plan is the *summary* or *financing* plan.[3] It is a written document specifically prepared to raise money for the venture. It contains certain key parts of the complete plan but is structured to be meaningful to those who may supply funds (venture capitalists, bankers, stockholders, etc.). The financing plan may be a bound document and frequently will be prepared in an esthetically appealing way. The preparation and construction of the complete business plan and the summary or financing plan will occupy the remaining chapters of this book.

SUMMARY AND CONCLUSIONS

A business plan is a written document describing the what, why, where, how, when, and who of developing and operating a new (or existing) venture. It consists of a complete business plan and a summary (financing) business plan. The complete plan will include a strategic plan (which is normally prepared for a period of several years) and an operating plan (which is usually prepared for the year immediately ahead).

Planning requires a disciplined approach. Discipline is particularly important to the busy entrepreneur in a start-up situation who may be tempted not to devote the necessary time and attention to this important function, both at the outset of his venture and on a continuing basis. Planning also requires leadership skills on the part of the entrepreneur to permit him to properly use and benefit from the knowledge and experience of his subordinates.

When the planning documents are completed, the entrepreneur will have a road map to follow in all major aspects of his venture. If it is followed and kept current, as changing conditions may require, the business plan will enhance the probability of success of the venture in a significant way.

---

[3] In this book, the terms "financing plan" and "financial plan" are employed to have two very different meanings, and it is important for the reader to keep them straight. The summary or financing plan is a document used to raise money. It includes many key parts of the complete plan (see Figure 2-5). The financial plan, on the other hand, is an integral part of the strategic and operating plans that determines what assets (inventory, receivables, plant, equipment, etc.) the firm will have to have in order to produce its products (services) and how these assets will be financed (borrowing, earnings retention, sale of stock, etc.). The financial plan is discussed in greater detail in the chapters to follow (particularly Chapters 4, 5, and 6). The results of the *financial* plan cue the entrepreneur that he needs to raise money and, hence, take his *financing* plan to investors.

KEY TERMS

Budget. A defined revenue and expense stream (usually over a 1-year period) resulting from a plan.

Business Plan. A narrative and quantitative statement describing the what, why, where, how, when, and who of developing and operating a new (or existing) venture.

Complete Business Plan. The entire planning document including an introduction, a summary of the key characteristics of the industry and proposed (existing) venture, *pro forma* financial statements, a complete analysis of the industry, the form and organizational structure of the venture, a strategic plan, an operating plan, and appendices including pertinent contracts, technical information, and supporting data. The complete business plan is a vital management tool for enhancing the chances for success of the new (or existing) enterprise.

Goals. General statements about why a business is formed (or continues to exist) and what is to be accomplished.

Management Functions. Planning, organizing, staffing, directing, and controlling.

Management Information System. A system designed to evaluate progress in execution of the plan and to assist in predicting, in comparing actual results with predictions, and in reducing deviations between predictions and actual results.

Market Theory of Management. A theory which views the role of management as reacting to events as they occur (crisis management).

Objectives. Concrete quantitative statements that are consistent with the goals of the enterprise.

Operating Plan. A document describing how to run the business effectively in the months (year) immediately ahead while progress is made towards the objectives of the strategic plan.

Planning and Control Theory of Management. A theory which considers the managerial role as being comprised of decisions and actions today that are forward-looking and which are based upon assessments of future expected developments. This concept rests upon the belief that the primary success factor in an enterprise is the competence of management to plan and control the activities of the business.

Pro Forma *Financial Statements.* Planned balance sheets, income statements, and cash flow analyses for each year of the planning period (with footnotes to explain the assumptions behind the figures).

Strategic Plan. A document describing what products and/or services the enterprise is going to offer to which class of customers in specified geographical areas. Strategic planning takes into account the broad goals of the organization and usually deals in horizons of several years.

Summary (Financing) Business Plan. Those parts of the complete plan which venture capitalists, bankers, and other financiers might wish to review prior to committing funds to the enterprise. It should include all elements of the complete plan except the strategic plan, the operating plan, and certain appendices.

REFERENCES

Ackoff, Russell L. *A Concept of Corporate Planning.* New York: John Wiley & Sons, Inc., 1972.

Ansoff, H. I., Declerck, R. P., and Hayes, R. L. *From Strategic Planning to Strategic Management.* New York: John Wiley & Sons, Inc., 1976.

Drucker, Peter F. *Management: Tasks, Responsibilities, Practices.* New York: Harper & Row, Inc., 1974.

Ekman, Jan: "The Scrapping of the Forecasts," *Euromoney,* October, 1981, pp. 222–229.

Ewing, David. *The Human Side of Planning.* New York: Macmillan Company, 1969.

——. *Long-Range Planning for Management.* New York: Harper & Row, Inc., 1972.

Hosmer, LaRue T., Cooper, Arnold C., and Vesper, Karl H. *The Entrepreneurial Function.* Englewood Cliffs, NJ: Prentice-Hall, Inc., 1977.

Hussey, David. *Corporate Planning.* Oxford, England: Pergamon Press, 1974.

——. *Introducing Corporate Planning.* Oxford, England: Pergamon Press, 1971.

Koontz, Harold, and O'Donnell, Cyril. *Principles of Management, An Analysis of Managerial Functions.* Fifth Ed. New York: McGraw-Hill Book Co., Inc., 1972.

Liles, Patrick R. *New Business Ventures and the Entrepreneur.* Homewood, IL: Richard D. Irwin, Inc., 1974.

McCarthy, Daniel J., Minichiello, Robert J., and Curran, Joesph R. *Business Policy and Strategy: Concepts and Readings.* Homewood, IL: Richard D. Irwin, Inc., 1975.

MacMillan, Ian C. *Strategy Formulation: Political Concepts.* St. Paul, MN: West Publishing Co., 1978.

Mockler, Robert J. *Business Planning and Policy Formation.* New York: Appleton-Century-Crofts, Inc., 1972.

O'Connor, Rochelle O. *Corporate Guides to Long-Range Planning.* New York: The Conference Board, 1976.

Osgood, William R. *Basics of Successful Business Planning.* New York: AMACOM, a division of American Management Associations, 1980.

Schoennauer, Alfred W.   *The Formulation and Implementation of Corporate Objectives and Strategies.* Oxford, OH: Planning Executives Institute, 1972.

Steiner, George A.   *Top Management Planning.* New York: Macmillan Company, 1969.

Taylor, Bernard, and Sparkes, John R.   *Corporate Strategy and Planning.* New York: Halsted Press, 1977.

Vesper, Karl H.   *New Venture Strategies.* Englewood Cliffs, NJ: Prentice-Hall, Inc., 1980.

3
Initial Steps in Preparing
the Business Plan

The purpose of this chapter is to provide the entrepreneur with a step-by-step guide, setting the foundation for writing a business plan. Each of these initial steps must be taken before the actual plan can be prepared. In Chapter 4, we will build upon the steps set forth below in order to create an actual plan.

In this chapter, a continuous example will be portrayed. By illustrating the details of plan preparation with a single example, you will see how a plan should be done from start to finish. The company chosen is a service business that is relatively easy to understand operationally. Our reason for selecting this kind of enterprise is so that we may discuss the basics of preparing the business plan without getting lost in minor details that would be of interest to only one industry or kind of business. Of course, detail knowledge of the specific characteristics of an enterprise is a necessary requirement for preparing a good plan, but there are too many types of businesses with unique features to illustrate even a few in a short, concise treatment such as the one we present here. Nevertheless, the example we have chosen perfectly reflects the economic nature of that business (a funeral home), and it should not be at all difficult for the entrepreneur to take the analysis and expand or change it where necessary for his own case. Also, samples of several additional business plans are provided in the Appendix to demonstrate alternative style and content procedures. Needless to say, plans will vary depending upon the nature of the business involved, the age of the business, and the purposes for which the plan is being prepared. In the example employed in the book (Chapters 3 through 6), it is assumed that the plan is for a new enterprise. The procedure for planning for an on-going enterprise would not be different, however.

THE JACKSON FUNERAL HOME

Ben Jackson is a prospective entrepreneur who is contemplating establishing a new business. He is 35 years old and has spent the past eight years as a funeral director in Newark. Given his experience and a "burning desire" to be the proprietor of his own business, he has begun the preparation of a business plan to determine whether the new venture makes economic sense. He intends to prepare a complete plan to assist him and his future employees guide the enterprise from its initiation through its first year and then on to the next three years of operations. The complete plan will then be summarized in a financing plan which will be used to raise the funds required to get the business started and see it through its first four years.

In early 1982, Ben began contemplating opening a business in Wesson, New Jersey, which is located north of Philadelphia just east of the Pennsylvania state line. His choice of location was based partly on his personal desire to live in a smaller town and partly on his belief that a new funeral home could be successful in Wesson. In making the location decision, it occurred to Ben that he was already in the process of planning. In fact, the process had actually started from the point that he decided to establish a new funeral concern.

STEP ONE: STATEMENT OF ENTERPRISE MISSION

There has to be a reason for a business to exist. For most businesses, there are probably a number of reasons that they exist. For many entrepreneurs, a business represents a means of self expression. It allows the entrepreneur a creative opportunity "to do your own thing." The business thus provides an important psychological raison d'être. Interestingly, this motivation for owning and operating an enterprise may be more important than the more obvious one: to make money. Nevertheless, making a profit usually plays a role in the decision to be in business, and few entities can exist for long if they do not become profitable at some point. There are many other explanations for the existence of a business as well, and it is critically important for the entrepreneur to ask himself from the start just *why* he wants to be in business.

The desire to have a business for whatever reason is not sufficient in and of itself to explain the justification for an enterprise. There also has to be an economic "demand" before a firm can survive. That is, the business must supply products or services that people will buy in sufficient quantity to justify the cost of producing those goods or services. The entrepreneur who says, "I want to be in the hobby shop business in Podunkville because I want 'to do my own thing' and I like the climate in Podunkville," may not be in business long if nobody in town wants to buy model airplanes and other products in the hobby shop line. On the other hand, there are many businesses that came into being because there was a real need for specific goods or services, and some smart entrepreneur came along to establish a firm to provide them.

The first step in business planning is the delineation of the reasons a given firm should exist. These reasons should be spelled out in a short, one- or two-sentence narrative statement (called the *Enterprise Mission*) that reflects the motivations of both the entrepreneur who creates (or sustains) the entity and the market which will be served by it (and hence will pay money for its products or services).

The Mission of the Jackson Funeral Home

Ben Jackson has given serious thought to the mission of his proposed new business. He has determined that there are two principal reasons that he wants to be in business for himself. First, he wants to have the freedom to determine how he lives his life. Thus far, while working for other people, his lifestyle and even the timing of his rising in the morning and going to bed in the evening has been determined by someone else. He would like to decide these things for himself in the future. Second, Ben wants to be financially independent. His first personal goal is to reach a net worth of a least $250,000 before he is 40 years old (five years hence).

Based upon his experience, Ben has also considered what the public wants from a funeral service firm. He knows that in time of personal bereavement the family needs assistance and services of a professional caliber, offered in dignified facilities and manner. He also knows that many people feel very vulnerable when dealing with funeral homes and funeral directors. They fear being "ripped off," yet few people would want to take care of many of the unpleasant tasks that are handled by the mortuary establishment. Thus, Ben has decided that he must build a reputation as an honorable and ethical businessman in order to gain the trust of his community.

Mission. To provide the Wesson area community with the highest quality funeral home facilities and services, while permitting the proprietor of the business to achieve personal and financial independence and pride in a sensitive service well performed.

STEP TWO: DEFINITION OF BUSINESS

It might seem like a simple enough matter to define what a business does, but is it really so easy? Years ago, Santa Fe Industries considered itself to be a railroad. Its name, the Atchison, Topeka, and Santa Fe Railway Company, signified that the firm carried people and freight by railway over given routes. Later, the AT&SF began to think of itself not as just a railroad but as a transportation company. The Santa Fe was in the business of transporting people and commodities. This broader definition encouraged the development of a range of transportation services to include trucking and pipelines. Now, Santa Fe Industries is a diversified company active in four major business areas: transportation, natural resources, forest products, and real estate and construction.[1]

The business definition should be broad enough to stimulate thinking and not constrain creativity but narrow enough to provide direction. Thus, it might be useful for an "oil" company to consider itself as an energy concern. Most major "oil" companies in the United States now deem themselves to be suppliers of all forms of energy and are either providing or are exploring the potential of supplying oil, gas, coal, solar energy, and other power sources. As business has become more complex and competitive in recent years, older definitions of businesses have become broader. Banks, for example, have established holding companies and are becoming

---

[1] Santa Fe Industries, Inc., *Annual Report,* 1980.

general financial service firms. Newspapers are really in the communications business, and stockbrokers are specialized financial service concerns. Interestingly, it is those industries where broader business definitions have been employed that have demonstrated the most growth and development. Less imaginative industries (steel, for example) that cling to the definitions more or less established around the turn of the twentieth century have shown less growth and many have entered a stage of absolute decline.

Definition of the Jackson Funeral Home

Years ago, cabinet makers began making speciality boxes (called coffins then) for burying the dead. This was a side activity that merely complemented the cabinet maker's other carpentry products. After a time, some cabinet makers began to concentrate exclusively on making burial boxes, and by the mid-nineteenth century individuals were setting up businesses to "undertake" to handle all the unpleasant details associated with the care and burial of the dead. These undertaking concerns found a demand for products and services in addition to burial boxes, and by the turn of the twentieth century funeral "parlors" were becoming common. They provided for the removal and transportation of the dead, cosmetology and embalming services, and a location to hold a funeral service. Modern funeral directors have come to realize that their principal role is not merely caring for the dead but tending to the needs of the family and friends of the dead person. Thus, services ranging from writing obituaries and helping the family with insurance and social security claims, to providing an on-the-premises psychologist who specializes in grief therapy, are becoming increasingly common. Ben Jackson is aware of the history and development of his industry and feels that anything less than a full-service funeral home would be unsuccessful. He is also aware of a countertrend toward very simple memorial services where the body is cremated and only a limited range of merchandise and services are demanded. In some communities (large cities, the West Coast, etc.), a limited service firm might be successful. He believes such a firm would not do well in the market he plans to enter.

Definition. The Jackson Funeral Home will be a full-service mortuary providing services and merchandise related to the care and disposition of the dead and assistance to their families in the area surrounding Wesson, New Jersey.

STEP THREE: IDENTIFICATION OF OPPORTUNITY

Once the entrepreneur has stated the mission of and defined his business, he must confirm that there is a need for the enterprise. Thus, in the case of new entity, he should spell out why the proposed firm should be started, what unique niche it will fill, and why someone else has not already done the same thing. For an existing entity, the entrepreneur should detail why the firm was needed originally, what niche it has been filling, and what (if any) competition has arisen and why. The initial formulation of a market analysis (which will later be incorporated into the business plan as part of the marketing plan and strategy) should be made. The entrepreneur may perform this task by himself, or he may engage a market analysis firm to handle the project. In any event, certain key economic, geographic, demographic, and other data will be required in the preparation of the market analysis.

The Jackson Funeral Home Opportunity

Ben Jackson has spent several months analyzing the market for funeral services in the greater Wesson area. He has prepared a "pin map" illustrating the residence locations of those dying in the city. The map identifies which of the existing funeral homes in Wesson handled each service for the past four years. He also secured the services of a market research firm that did a demographic study of the market area in question. The report of Market Analysis, Inc., is shown in Figure 3-1. Ben has concluded that there is a definite need for a new funeral firm in Wesson to replace the old Second Avenue Mortuary (see discussion in Figure 3-1). He believs a minimum of 100 services could be secured (only a 3.3% share of the market) with no marketing effort and that figure could double over the next decade if a consistent effort were made to appeal to families who presently employ the services of other funeral directors in the city.

The city of Wesson is located in New Jersey north of Philadelphia and east of the Pennsylvania state line. The median income in the city has risen from $15,200 per year in 1978 to $20,200 per year in 1981. The recorded population estimates for the city are as follows:

1978 — 320,000
1979 — 318,000
1980 — 315,000
1981 — 310,000

The slight decline in population reflects a migration to the suburbs over the past 6 years. Most of the migration has been to the north and northwest, outside the Wesson city limits and is thus not reflected in the figures. Overall population of the county is approximately 425,000. The northwest area has been growing at a rate exceeding the losses from Wesson. Furthermore, whereas the median income within the city is lower than the national average, these newer suburbs are much more affluent.

Our survey indicates, however, that the people who proportionately spend the most on funerals, nationally, are not the wealthiest. The distribution for sales of services by income level is skewed below the national income average. Of additional interest is our finding that the death rate within the city of Wesson is higher than the national average; 10 deaths per thousand in 1978, down to 9.8 deaths per thousand in 1981. These figures reflect the same trend, however, as national statistics toward a lower death rate per thousand over the last few years.

Wesson Mortality Statistics

1978 — 3,200 deaths
1979 — 3,120 deaths
1980 — 3,092 deaths
1981 — 3,038 deaths

There are no funeral sales figures available for the northern areas as yet, but only 2 funeral homes are operating there at the moment.

Conclusions drawn are that the migrating and new population influxes to the north and northwest are middle class, more affluent families. In contrast, it would seem from the higher than average death rates, that the city of Wesson has an older, more established population with slightly lower income base. Wesson currently has a predominantly Christian population with 65% of these persons being Protestant and 35% Catholic. Approximately 30% of the city is Black.

Although the central downtown area has deteriorated in recent years, and is the predominantly Black area, real estate values in the past six months have risen. A partial explanation is that new home construction in the northern areas has slowed down in the past several months as high interest rates have dried up available mortgage money. There are, instead, isolated instances of old Victorian houses being rehabilitated within the city because they have been available at bargain prices. There appears to be little concern by these few returning families about the condition of the homes or the minority dominance in the neighborhoods.

A second, equally plausible explanation seems to be the energy crisis. More and more houses in the central area are being sold to former commuters from the suburbs. Whether businesses shall follow them in this return to the central district is anyone's guess at this

Figure 3-1. Report of Market Analysis, Inc.

point. Although no conclusions can be drawn from the tenuous evidence, indicators do reveal that the average sales price of the older homes has risen 15% in the past 6 months.

The funeral home businesses in Wesson are all locally owned and operated. Two have been in business nearly 50 years; and one (The Wesson Mortuary) is clearly the superior location in the city, as supported by both the sales figures among the competitors and by several interviews we conducted with local civic leaders. [See Attachments 1 and 2. (Omitted)]

There are currently 12 funeral homes operating in Wesson, down from 13 last year. Three of these funeral homes serve the Black community primarily. As mentioned, not included in the total are two additional funeral homes opened in the northern area within the past year. [See Attachment 3 for a map of the funeral homes and cemeteries locations. (Omitted)]

An analysis of the pin map supplied to us by Mr. B. Jackson suggests the possible need for a new funeral location to replace the mortuary that closed last year. That firm was located on Second Avenue, downtown, and served an increasingly elderly market. The business did not fail, but was closed by the widow of the former owner. It is our understanding that the property and physical location can be purchased. In past years, the Second Avenue Mortuary handled about 100 services per year with no marketing effort. Surveys indicate that families selected Second Avenue principally because of its convenient location.

Figure 3-1. Report of Market Analysis, Inc. (continued)

STEP FOUR: SPECIFICATION OF EXTERNAL VARIABLES

The next step in laying the foundation for writing the formal business plan is to specify those factors outside the control of the business that will affect its success. Current data about these variables should be collected and analyzed.

Where do you get information about external variables? Probably the most widely discussed external variable is the Gross National Product (GNP). Nevertheless, most businesses are not big enough to be directly influenced by GNP. General Motors may worry when GNP is down 5%, but there are many other economic, demographic, and social statistics that may be more important to the average business. Many of these data are available in numerous government publications which are reasonably priced. Most of these publications are available in U.S. Government Book Stores that are located throughout the country. These stores have practically everything the government prints, and if they do not have a particular item they will order it for you.

A very important source is the *Statistical Abstract*. This is an excellent compilation of data in simplified, abstract form; and it also contains references which indicate the source of original information. The *Statistical Abstract* is published annually and costs about $13 hardcover and $10 paperback. It has a wide variety of factual and useful statistical information.

Every five years a *Census of Business* is taken covering sales, employees, payroll, etc., of almost every category of business. Censuses are available for many years past and thus can provide information regarding long-run trends for various types of businesses. Similarly, the use of data from the demographic census taken each decade may be useful. For many businesses, demographic factors (such as population, age groupings, income levels, etc.) are important and this type of information can be obtained for small areas called "census tracts." Also, the local Chamber of Commerce is frequently an excellent source of economic, statistical, and other information, and many of the larger banks have substantial data files as well.

Another recommended source is the *U.S. Industrial Outlook*, an annual publication of the Department of Commerce which examines practically every industry in the U.S. and makes economic projections. *The Economic Report of the President* is required reading for those who need such economic data as GNP, consumer price indexes, interest rates, etc. The Small Business Administration is yet another source of information. They supply free (or at nominal cost) booklets on everything from how to establish an accounting system for your firm to how to price your product. Some of these publications are limited in scope and detail, but they are worth having. The Internal Revenue Service and the various state comptroller's Offices also can be sources of information. They publish tax guide materials and provide tax assistance to businesses.

The Wall Street Journal is an outstanding source of current information on national and international problems and trends affecting business. Other excellent publications are *Business Week, Forbes,* and *Fortune. The Economist* is an important international publication, and it is worth reading for the perspective it provides on international issues as well as on events in the United States. Years ago what happened in certain distant countries like Iran did not make too much difference to us, but they do now. There are all kinds of international dislocations and problems that can affect your business.

Obviously, a businessman cannot absorb all the information and knowledge available in these multiple sources. However, the well informed entrepreneur must learn what to read and how to read it quickly to get information that may have an impact on his business. This is integral to planning and to managing an enterprise. Many of the dreams, ideas, and thoughts for new businesses probably incubated from something read by an entrepreneur.

External Variables Affecting the Jackson Funeral Home

In analyzing the Jackson Funeral Home opportunity, Ben Jackson considered the major external variables that might affect his business. The report of Market Analysis, Inc., suggested that certain economic, demographic, social, and competitive variables might be significant. Among these were: (1) the median income levels of families residing in Wesson, (2) total population and population movements in Wesson, (3) the mortality rate and absolute number of deaths in Wesson, (4) the religious and ethnic mix of the population, and (5) the number and location of other funeral homes in Wesson. The report provided specific data about these variables for the four previous years. The next step in preparing the business plan will be to project values for the major variables for the forthcoming years.

There is an additional major category of variables that must be considered at least qualitatively; that is, the activities and policies of various governmental regulatory entities. The funeral home business is specifically regulated by the states, and most states license funeral directors and embalmers before they can practice. Ben is licensed in New Jersey and anticipates no difficulties in complying with any state regulations that might be imposed. Recently, however, the federal government has become interested in the business practices of funeral homes. The Federal Trade Commission has investigated the industry and found that some funeral homes engage in "unfair and deceptive" practices. Ben has read in the numerous trade magazines that he receives that the FTC may issue a Rule that would allow the federal government to determine how he could establish his prices, what kind of caskets he would have to offer to his customers, whether or not he could embalm and under what circumstances, and a host of other red-tape–type regulations that have come to characterize much of the federal regulatory apparatus over the past several decades. Ben is convinced that such federal intrusion is generally unnecessary and unwarranted since state regulation exists to determine when a licensee has been unscrupulous and to discipline him accordingly. Ben also believes that many Americans are fed up with the intrusion of the federal government in their lives and in the 1980 federal election voted out many of the "liberal politicians" who allowed the regulators to multiply. He agrees with a spokesman from a major funeral home trade association who has said, "The FTC will not issue a Rule, or if one is issued, it will have no perceptible impact on the operation of legitimate American funeral homes." Thus, Ben is making no provision in his business plan for the regulation of his business by the federal government. Should political conditions change and should it appear that the recent conservative trend evidenced in the United States may be arrested, Ben has decided that he may have to adjust his plan. He foresees no major difficulties with complying with any reasonable regulations, although he would expect to pass along to the customer any cost increases that might be associated with complying with federal regulations.

STEP FIVE: MAKING CRITICAL ASSUMPTIONS

Once the significant external variables have been determined and the pertinent sources of information have been located, it is necessary to make specific assumptions about each variable and project values for each period in the planning horizon. Ordinarily, this is the most difficult part of planning. Nevertheless, the major factors must be identified, and using whatever data that can be reasonably collected (plus the good judgment of the entrepreneur), an assumption should be made about each one.

To whatever extent possible, the entrepreneur should employ projections that have already been made by experts in the field in question, although these might be tempered with his own view of the situation. For example, if macroeconomic statistics are important external data to a given industry, the forecasts of various economists might be used as a starting point for projections. Forecasts of GNP, consumer prices, interest rates, and other such economic data are made by many economists and appear regularly in business publications. It is, of course, true that economists are frequently wrong and they often disagree violently among themselves about what is going to happen in the future (and what is happening now, for that matter), but their professional views are probably sounder than the seat-of-the-pants prognostication of the entrepreneur who has never read an economics text. Nevertheless, judgment should play the deciding role, and the entrepreneur has to feel convinced that the position of the experts fits his own situation and is pertinent.

Forecasts are provided by many governmental agencies for all sorts of data. The *U.S. Industrial Outlook* has previously been referred to as a useful source. In addition, the Labor Department also provides helpful projections on data such as labor force and price trends. For the smaller concern operating in a limited area, however, forecasts on a national basis may be of little value and local economic factors should be assessed. For example, some areas of the country (such as Houston, Texas) continue to enjoy boom conditions while other areas suffer a recession. Fortunately, most of the banks and the Chambers of Commerce in the larger cities maintain data files and projections on important economic, demographic, and competitive conditions in their communities. The entrepreneur should consult these sources in preparing his projections.

Finally, the entrepreneur does not have to reinvent the wheel when he plans. There are a number of consultants and professional data analysis firms that specialize in gathering information and making projections about essential statistical series. The entrepreneur might find that spending two or three thousand dollars to get an outsider to help him analyze the exogenous variables affecting his business is an excellent investment. It would cost him far more in time if he tried to do the same thing, assuming he had the expertise in the first place. Also, do not overlook the possibility of hiring a professor from a nearby university economics department or business school as a consultant. While the days when these professionals would work for practically the minimum wage are behind us, most of them have their overhead (offices, secretaries, etc.) already covered and can provide exceptional services for reasonable fees.

Critical Assumptions about the Jackson Funeral Home

Ben Jackson has decided that a four-year time horizon will be the appropriate planning period for his new business. With this in mind, he has reviewed the pertinent data series gathered for him by Market Analysis, Inc. The most important information relates to the expected demand for his services, and population and mortality statistics are those most germane to project such demand. He has summarized these data as shown in Table 3-1, page 40.

Ben also knows, however, that funeral services are provided along ethnic and racial lines. Although no ethical (or profit-oriented) funeral home would discriminate against a family on racial or religious grounds, it is usually the case that White Protestants use one funeral home, Black Protestants another, White Catholics still another, and Jewish people still another. In very large cities, such as New York, the specialization may get even more pronounced with one funeral home catering to Orthodox Jews while another handles primarily Conservative and Reformed congregations. Ben is a White Presbyterian and believes that most of his business will come from White Protestants although he may get some business from White Catholics. He expects his Black and Jewish clientele to be nominal. Given this added information, Ben has asked Market Analysis, Inc., to investigate the demographic characteristics in the seven census tracts falling within a three-mile radius of the proposed location of the Jackson Funeral Home on Second Avenue. The material in Table 3-2 was subsequently supplied.

These data suggest that the overall population in the determined market area has declined slightly over the past four years (by 3.5%), but the percentage of Protestant and Catholic Whites has risen

Table 3-1
Demographic Data on Wesson, New Jersey

Year	Population	Number of Mortalities	Mortality Rate (per thousand)
1978	320,000	3,200	10.0
1979	318,000	3,120	9.8
1980	315,000	3,092	9.8
1981	310,000	3,038	9.8

Table 3-2
Demographic Data on Area Surrounding the
Proposed Location of the Jackson Funeral Home

Year	Population	Protestant Whites	Catholic Whites	Other
1978	31,500	20,200	6,400	4,900
1979	31,300	20,100	6,300	4,900
1980*	30,498	19,603	6,212	4,683
1981	30,400	19,600	6,200	4,600

*The population figure for 1980 is taken from the U.S. Census which is taken every 10 years. The figures for the other years are extrapolations based on prior censuses and observed trends in the census tracts surveyed.

(from 84.4% to 84.9%). Thus, the population of the determined market has declined by a smaller percentage (3.0%) than the population as a whole.

Next, Ben asked Market Analysis, Inc., to analyze the age structure of the population in the seven census tracts. Since the death rate among the elderly is far higher than for younger people, he deemed such data to be highly significant. It was determined that over half of the population in the area in question was over age fifty and that 20% were above age sixty-five. This is much different from the aggregate U.S. statistic (about 11% over age 65) and somewhat different from the aggregate Wesson figure. Interestingly, it turned out that although only about 10% of Wesson's population lived in the seven census tracts in question, 15% of the population over age sixty-five lived there, and 21% of White Protestant and Catholics over age sixty-five were residents of the area.

The final step in the demographic analysis was to examine the mortality statistics for the seven census tracts. It was not possible to break these data down along racial and religious lines, but it was possible to determine the number of services handled by the old Second Avenue Mortuary and compare this figure with the total number of mortalities (see Tables 3-3 and 3-4).

Table 3-3
Mortality Data on Area Surrounding the
Proposed Location of the Jackson Funeral Home

Year	Population	Number of Mortalities	Mortality Rate (per thousand)
1978	31,500	397	12.6
1979	31,300	388	12.4
1980	30,498	369	12.1
1981	30,400	374	12.3

Table 3-4
Mortality Data and Market Share of
Second Avenue Mortuary

Year	Number of Mortalities	Services Handled by Second Avenue	Percentage
1978	397	126	31.7
1979	388	110	28.4
1980	369	98	26.6
1981	374	no longer in business	—

Given these data, Market Analysis, Inc. has projected the potential total market and the possible share that Jackson might hope to attain over the next four years. It was assumed that the small population decline would continue and that the mortality rate would stabilize at around 12.2 per thousand. These data are shown in Table 3-5.

Ben considered the other major external variables that might be significant to his business and determined that income levels and the consumer price index (CPI) might influence what families were willing to spend on funeral services. He also gathered data from the leading trade association in his business to find out what the trend in per service expenditures had been for the most recent four-year period that data were available. The figures in Table 3-6 were compiled.

After consulting with Market Analysis, Inc., it was decided that there was some correlation between median family income, the CPI, and per service funeral expenditures. A regression equation of per

Table 3-5
Total Market for Funeral Services and
Possible Share of Jackson Funeral Home
1982-1986

Year	Population	Mortality Rate (per thousand)	Mortalities	Percentage Handled by Jackson	Case Volume Expected by Jackson
1982*	30,350	12.2	370	—	—
1983	30,300	12.2	370	25.0	93
1984	30,200	12.2	368	27.0	99
1985	30,100	12.2	367	30.0	110
1986	30,000	12.2	366	35.0	128

*Year in progress.

Table 3-6
Pertinent Economic Data
Jackson Funeral Home
1978-1981

Year	Median Family Income	Consumer Price Index (All Items)	Per Service Funeral Expenditures Nation-wide
1978	$17,640	195.3	$ 1,412
1979	19,661	217.7	1,429
1980	21,023	247.0	1,503
1981	22,284	272.3	1,596

service expenditure nationwide (PSE) and median family income (MFI) was performed and the following was found:[2]

$$PSE = 566 + (0.045)(MFI)$$

Similarly, a regression equation was fitted for per service expenditure and the CPI:

$$PSE = 887 + (2.5)(CPI)$$

Given these results, Market Analysis, Inc., projected the per service expenditure nationwide for the next five years as follows:

1982	$1,620
1983	1,670
1984	1,720
1985	1,790
1986	1,850

Jackson was cautioned, however, that data for Wesson might not be identical to those nationwide and that local statistics on incomes, prices, and per service funeral expenditures should be secured before he attempted to forecast his expected revenue per service. Market Analysis was commissioned to get these data for Mr. Jackson prior to his structuring of the complete business plan (Chapter 4).

STEP SIX: PINPOINTING SUCCESS DETERMINANTS

The next step in laying the foundation for writing the formal business plan is to pinpoint the important internal variables that affect successful performance. What are the major factors? For some firms, the growth rate of sales will be the most important element. These enterprises usually have some degree of control over the

---

[2] An explanation of the technique of regression analysis is beyond the scope of this book. Practically any elementary statistics book would provide a discussion of the subject. See, for example, Chapter 12 of Clark, Charles T., and Schkade, Lawrence L. *Statistical Analysis for Administrative Decisions.* Cincinnati, OH: South-Western Publishing Co., 1979.

market in which they participate, and an aggressive advertising and sales promotion program may be the key to success. Other companies face a more competitive situation where they may be unable to secure a larger market share by adopting an aggressive selling strategy. These firms may even have their prices set by a market dominated by larger competitors or customers who may be able to dictate terms. The major success determinants for such entities may be those relating to cost control and efficiency.

Each particular business will have its unique mix of key internal variables. For manufacturing firms, turnovers, rejects, machine downtime, and capacity may be quite important. For service entities, labor costs, account collection, and overhead control may be significant. Retail concerns usually must be very aware of mark-ups, inventory management, and promotional techniques. Businesses of all kinds with high fixed cost levels must be knowledgeable of their cost structure and the dollar and unit break-even points.

There are a number of variables which influence the riskiness of the total enterprise.[3] The most significant of these variables is the predictability of a firm's revenues. If the entrepreneur knows with a high degree of confidence the level of sales for a number of years in advance, the planning process is facilitated. Furthermore, knowledge of future revenues allows the entrepreneur to arrange disbursements without fear of possible financial embarrassment. Although a firm's revenue pattern may be highly volatile over time, if the nature of the volatility is known with certainty, the planning process can reduce the impact of fluctuations. On the other hand, if revenues are volatile and unpredictable, no amount of planning can abate the consequences of volatility.

A volatile sales pattern implies a highly uncertain flow of cash into the firm. This is disadvantageous for two reasons: (1) a risky pattern of cash inflows may reduce the ability of the firm to meet its cash payment obligations, and (2) a risky pattern of cash inflows will generally result in an unstable pattern of net income.[4] In the first

---

[3] The balance of the material in this section is adapted, with permission of the publisher, from Findlay, M. Chapman, III, and Williams, Edward E. *An Integrated Analysis for Managerial Finance.* Englewood Cliffs, NJ: Prentice-Hall, Inc., 1970, pp. 31–34.

[4] A corollary disadvantage associated with a highly uncertain flow of cash into the firm is that penalties may be imposed when cash deficiencies develop. For example, a firm may be forced to borrow on unfavorable terms or, more significantly, to liquidate assets. The result may be quite costly to the firm even though it would be able to meets its payments obligations.

instance, risky cash inflows increase the possibility of insolvency; in the second, they may reduce the value of the business.

Although the most important determinant of the riskiness of an enterprise is the predictability of its revenues, there are other variables which may magnify the impact of a volatile cash inflow pattern. One such variable is the degree of *operating leverage* characteristic of the firm. A firm possessing a high degree of operating leverage is characterized by high operating fixed costs. Operating fixed costs include such items as depreciation, overhead, permanent salaries, etc. The presence of high operating fixed costs may increase the possibility of insolvency, since fixed costs do not vary with output, and will increase the volatility of earnings. (Noncash charges, such as depreciation, may influence the volatility of earnings, but they will not increase the probability of the firm's running short of cash.) Let us assume a business faced with the following set of sales possibilities:

	Sales
Maximum expectation	$150,000
Most likely expectation	100,000
Minimum expectation	50,000

Let us further assume that the business has a *variable cost ratio* (variable cost/sales) of 0.8 and operating fixed costs of $20,000. In the best of all possible worlds, where sales are $150,000, the firm's income statement would be as follows:

Sales		$150,000
Variable costs	$120,000	
Operating fixed costs	20,000	140,000
Earnings		$ 10,000

If sales are only $100,000, however, the business just breaks even:

Sales		$100,000
Variable costs	$80,000	
Operating fixed costs	20,000	100,000
Earnings		$ 0

In the worst of all possible worlds, where sales are $50,000:

Sales		$ 50,000
Variable costs	$ 40,000	
Operating fixed costs	20,000	60,000
Earnings		($ 10,000)

Thus, the presence of operating fixed costs in the third instance would result in a net loss for the firm.

Operating leverage is frequently examined in terms of *break-even analysis*. The break-even point is defined as that level of sales where revenues exactly equal expenses. Fixed costs play a crucial role in break-even analysis, since a firm with no fixed costs would have a break-even sales point of zero. The variable cost ratio is also significant, since a firm's contribution to fixed costs (and profit beyond the break-even point) depends on how much of an extra dollar of sales must go to meet variable costs. In the above example, the variable cost ratio is 0.8. Thus, every additional sales dollar provides a $0.20 contribution to fixed costs and profit. In the case of a fixed cost level of $20,000, sales must be $100,000 to break even. Every dollar of sales less than $100,000 means a loss of $0.20. On the other hand, every dollar of sales over $100,000 means a profit of $0.20. These relationships are described in the following equation:

$$S_b = \frac{FC}{1 - \dfrac{VC}{S}}$$

where:

S_b is break-even sales
FC is the volume of operating fixed costs
VC is the variable cost per unit of sales
S is the selling price per unit

It is unnecessary to know the break-even volume in terms of units for most purposes. In the variable cost ratio, the unit expression drops out. Thus, if the selling price is $10 per unit and the variable cost per unit is $8, the VC ratio is 0.8. This ratio could also have been determined from an income statement by comparing total variable costs to total sales.

In order to explore the impact of operating leverage on the riskiness of the enterprise a bit further, let us consider another example. Assume that a firm has a high degree of operating leverage. Let VC/S = 0.2 and operating fixed costs equal $80,000. The break-even point for this entity would be:

$$S_b = \frac{\$80,000}{1 - 0.2} = \$100,000$$

Thus, the break-even point for this firm is the same as for the company in the previous example. The firms are distinctly different, however, in that the latter firm is far more leveraged operationally. Let us assume several possible sales levels with the ensuing income statements for the latter enterprise:

Sales	$120,000	$140,000	$160,000
VC	24,000	28,000	32,000
FC	80,000	80,000	80,000
Earnings	$ 16,000	$ 32,000	$ 48,000

Let us further assume that $140,000 is the expected sales figure but that there is a possibility that sales could be $120,000 or $160,000. If sales turned out to be $160,000, actual sales would have exceeded expected sales by $20,000, or $20,000/$140,000 = 14.3%. Earnings, however, would have been $16,000 larger, or $16,000/$32,000 = 50%! This percentage difference in earnings, given any change in sales, is the essence of operating leverage. Leverage may also work unfavorably. Had sales been 14.3% under the estimate ($120,000 instead of $140,000), earnings would have been cut in half! These examples illustrate the effects of operating leverage given differences in actual sales from expected sales. Similar examples could illustrate changes in earnings given changes in actual sales over time. Of course, if these sales changes were known with certainty, the earnings stream could also be predicted with certainty.

Returning to our initial example where VC/S = 0.8 and operating fixed costs are $20,000, let us assume a profit of $32,000 as in the previous case. The projected income statement would be:

Sales	$260,000
VC	208,000
FC	20,000
Earnings	$ 32,000

Now, let us vary sales positively and negatively by 14.3% as in the previous example (14.3% × $260,000 = $37,200):

Sales	$222,800	$260,000	$297,200
VC	178,240	208,000	237,760
FC	20,000	20,000	20,000
Earnings	$ 24,560	$ 32,000	$ 39,440

The change in earnings, given a sales change of 14.3%, is $7,440, or $7,440/$32,000 = 23.3%. Thus, the leverage factor is roughly half of that in the previous case.

Success Determinants for the Jackson Funeral Home

Ben Jackson's basic knowledge of funeral home operations has enabled him to determine the important internal economic variables that will spell success or failure for his new venture. Despite the fact that a funeral home is essentially a service business, the large investment required to operate a funeral establishment means that it will typically have a low variable-cost-to-sales ratio and a high level of fixed costs.[5] Most funeral homes also have substantial excess capacity which must be maintained to meet peak-load periods of demand. Salaries, which for all intents and purposes are a fixed cost for a funeral home, are usually the most significant expense item. Industry sources indicate that about 40% of the revenues of American funeral homes are spent on wages and salaries. Facility expenses (rent, taxes, depreciation, interest, utilities, maintenance, etc.) account for another 15%, while vehicles (lease costs, depreciation, interest, maintenance, gasoline, etc.) require about 12%. The most important variable cost item is casket merchandise, and this expense

---

[5] Most service businesses require only a small investment and hence have a low level of fixed costs (and hence a low break-even point).

accounts for about 18% of the funeral revenue dollar. Thus, a typical common-size income statement for a funeral home would appear as follows:[6]

Revenues		100%
Variable costs		
Merchandise	18%	
Fixed costs		
Salaries	40	
Facilities	15	
Vehicles	12	
Total costs		85
Profit before income tax		15%

The variable cost ratio for the typical establishment would be:

$$VC/S = 18/100 = 0.18$$

and the break-even point would depend on the overall level of fixed costs.

Of course, all fixed costs are only fixed in the short-run and for a range of volume. For example, it might be possible to handle between 0 and 200 services with a location of a given size, with a given number of employees and with a given number of vehicles. In the volume range from 200 to 500 services, a larger location, more people, and additional vehicles might be required. All businesses are similar in this respect in that fixed costs *may vary* as the size of the operation

---

[6] A common-size statement is one that is presented in percentages rather than absolute dollars. A common-size income statement expresses all cost items (and profit) as a percentage of sales. If a firm had sales of $80,000, variable cost of $10,000, fixed costs of $50,000 and profits of ($80,000 - $10,000 - $50,000) = $20,000, it would have a common-size income statement as follows:

Sales		100.0%	($80,000)
Variable costs	12.5%		($10,000/$80,000)
Fixed costs	62.5		($50,000/$80,000)
Total costs		75	($60,000/$80,000)
Profit		25%	($20,000/$80,000)

increases. Thus, it is important to determine the *relevant range* of business volume anticipated in preparing any plan. Obviously, because of the high fixed cost nature of the funeral business, volume becomes a key success variable in determining profitability. Large locations may spread fixed costs over more cases and thus get increasing income per dollar of revenue and invested capital. Ben Jackson considers his proposed location to be "typical" since his volume expectations are in line with those of the nation as a whole. Trade statistics indicate that the "average" American funeral home handles approximately 140 services annually, and the common-size income statement previously outlined is for a firm doing about this volume of business.

Although the level of fixed costs for the typical funeral home is high, this does not necessarily imply that funeral homes have a high degree of operating leverage. Actually, the contrary is true. Cash flows in the industry are stable due to the nature of the business, and bankruptcy is very rare. According to Dun & Bradstreet, funeral homes have a consistent record of suffering the fewest failures of any business in the United States.

STEP SEVEN: OUTLINING MAJOR STRENGTHS

The entrepreneur should next outline the major strengths of his venture idea which will provide the basis for success. What are the strengths? For some businesses, it will be the provision of a new product that has no competitive alternative. For others, it will be selling a product similar to others on the market for a lower price. For yet others, better service or a higher quality product will be the major strength of the endeavor.

The entrepreneur himself may be a key asset to his business. His knowledge, expertise, and overall "get-up-and-go" may be the most important success ingredient to the enterprise. In other cases, it may be the lack of expertise or entrepreneurship displayed by the competition that provides the principal strength of a venture. In a typical situation, the established firms tend to get conservative and fat and lazy thereby opening up an opportunity for someone else who will go that extra mile to provide better service or a superior product.

Occasionally, the marketing strategy of the entrepreneur will be his principal strength. He (or those whom he employs) may have prepared a superb advertising program or lined-up a larger network of distributors or carved out a unique niche in a highly specialized market. Location will sometimes play a role here. As in real estate acquisitions, there used to be an old saying in marketing that there are three reasons for the success of a retail establishment: location, location, and location.

Other strengths may be found in the following: (1) The financial capacity of the enterprise, (2) the ability of the entity to grant credit terms to customers, (3) the lack of indebtedness of the business, (4) the cost effectiveness and efficiency of the plant and equipment, (5) the age of the plant and equipment, (6) the employees who work for the firm, (7) the lack of a union among the employees, (8) existing contracts or the promise of contracts from major customers, (9) the financial condition of the clients of the business, and (10) the general economic climate at the time the planning period begins.

Of course, each situation will be different and the strengths for one situation will not apply to another. Nevertheless, the entrepreneur should be quite careful in outlining his existing and potential strengths. They will quite literally explain whether or not his business will succeed.

Major Strenghts of the Jackson Funeral Home

Ben Jackson has thought about the conceivable major strengths of his proposed new business. In order of importance, he has listed the following:

1. Location. The Jackson Funeral Home will be conveniently located on Second Avenue in a building that was formerly a reasonably successful funeral home.
2. Service. The Jackson Funeral Home will offer a full line of funeral merchandise (caskets, grave vaults, clothing, etc.) and will strive to offer the best service available in Wesson.
3. Price. The Jackson Funeral Home will price its merchandise and service to offer the best value in Wesson. The principal clientele of the firm will be elderly people with limited wealth. The families of these people should appreciate being able to get the best in quality for a reasonable price.

4. Building. The old Second Avenue Mortuary building will be completely remodeled to reflect an image of quality yet not opulence.
5. Employees. The Jackson Funeral Home will not be unionized. Employees will be personally selected by Ben Jackson from the most dependable people he has worked with throughout New Jersey and New York.

STEP EIGHT: OUTLINING MAJOR WEAKNESSES

The final step prior to the actual preparation of the planning documents is to outline the major weaknesses of the business that may cause it to fail. In many respects, outlining weaknesses is the reverse of outlining the strengths. Is the product or service not really very much differentiated from other products or services on the market? This may be a fatal weakness. Is the competition so severe that it may be difficult to carve out a unique niche in the market? This also may be a key weakness. Is it impossible to find just the right location? For a business that sells to the general public, this may be very significant.

For many new enterprises, the major weaknesses revolve around the lack of longevity of the firm. People simply do not know you are in business. This can be overcome in some instances by an aggressive marketing strategy, but it still takes time for the customer list to be developed. Building relationships with suppliers can also take time (and be costly) as older customers get preferred treatment at the expense of the new entrepreneur. Similiarly, the employees of the new enterprise may not be as skilled or experienced, at least initially, and this may lead to production, delivery, or selling errors. Over time, these problems can be remedied, but the firm has to have the financial resources to stay in business in the meanwhile.

Financial factors are often among the major weaknesses of the new enterprise. The firm may be undercapitalized and the financial needs of the business may have been seriously understated by the optimistic entrepreneur who was positive the firm would cross the break-even point during the second month of operations. The firm may have been started with a lot of borrowed money, and simply paying interest on the debt may be a problem. It may be difficult for the new business to get credit, and even suppliers may put the new enterprise on a C.O.D.[7] basis until it has been in business for awhile. Once again, each situation will be unique and the major weaknesses of one may not be at all applicable to another. Complete candor in analyzing the possible weaknesses of the new venture idea may be the most important element in preparing the business plan.

Major Weaknesses of the Jackson Funeral Home

Like most entrepreneurs, Ben Jackson does not like to think about the possibility that his new business will not be successful. Nevertheless, in being honest with himself and his financial backers, Ben has outlined the potential problem areas that he must face. Pinpointing these areas of weakness not only gives Ben a better idea about his chances for success, it also makes it possible for him to concentrate on curing any weaknesses that might exist. In order of importance, he has listed the following:

1. Nature of business. It typically takes a long time for a new funeral home to become established in the eyes of the community. Some businesses require months before they handle even a few services, and it may take years for a new location to become profitable.
2. Marketing strategy. It is difficult to market funerals. The nature of the service limits the effectiveness of the usual techniques such as a grand-opening sale or extensive advertising. Price cutting also does not work ordinarily, since people are not likely to buy a funeral simply because it has been marked down in price.
3. Competition. There are currently twelve funeral homes in Wesson. Although it appears that the market could support another one (particularly in the location that has been selected for the Jackson Funeral Home), competition would remain

---

[7]Cash on delivery. When goods are received C.O.D., they must be paid for as soon as they arrive. After a firm has been in business for awhile, credit terms are usually extended. Net 30 is a typical arrangement whereby goods are delivered and the purchaser then has 30 days from the time of arrival (or even the time of billing which may follow arrival by several days) before he has to pay. Discounts are sometimes offered to encourage prompt payment. Terms of 2/10 Net 30, for example, would allow the buyer to deduct two percent of the purchase price as a prompt payment discount if payment was made within ten days. Otherwise, full payment would be due in 30 days.

keen. Two competitors have been in business for over fifty years, and The Wesson Mortuary is clearly thought by almost everyone to be the prestige "carriage-trade" operation in the city. It is also the fastest growing business. Fortunately, it is located eight miles from the proposed site of the Jackson Funeral Home.

4. Market size. The population of Wesson has been decreasing in recent years and the death rate has been declining. As a result, the overall size of the market has been diminishing slightly.

5. Financing. Ben Jackson only has a limited amount of personal savings to invest in the business. Given what it will take to get the business started and sustained for the first year, additional funds will have to be borrowed or equity partners will have to be found.

SUMMARY AND CONCLUSIONS

The initial steps in setting the foundation for the complete business plan are critical to the plan's development. These steps provide the information and basis upon which the complete plan is built and help determine the degree of success the venture will have.

By way of a practical example, this chapter has demonstrated the thinking, actions, and analysis an entrepreneur should initially follow in developing a business plan. The critical steps include: (1) delineating the reasons and motivation for the entrepreneur to go into business for himself (resulting in a statement of the mission of the business); (2) describing the history of the industry (leading to the definition of the business); (3) identifying the business opportunity (market analysis); (4) specifying the external variables affecting the enterprise; (5) making critical assumptions about the variables and projecting values for them over the planning period; (6) pinpointing success determinants and projecting values for the internal variables that will affect success; (7) outlining major strengths; and (8) outlining major weaknesses.

With these initial steps completed, we are now ready to proceed to the preparation of the complete plan.

KEY TERMS

Break-Even Analysis.   Determining the level of sales revenues which exactly equals the sum of variable and fixed costs.

Critical Assumptions.   Projected values for each variable in the planning framework.

Common-size Statement.   Financial statements reduced to percentage terms.

Enterprise Definition.   A statement about what the firm will do.

Enterprise Major Strengths.   Elements that may provide the bases for the success of the enterprise.

Enterprise Major Weaknesses.   Elements that may result in the failure of the enterprise.

Enterprise Mission.   A delineation of the reasons for the existence of the firm.

Enterprise Opportunity Identification.   A market analysis designed to determine whether or not a proposed venture is feasible.

External Variables.   Factors outside the control of the entrepreneur which will affect the success of the enterprise.

Fixed Costs.   Costs that do not vary with changes in volume.

Operating Leverage.   The percentage magnification of net income and net cash flow as sales change (a result of the presence of operating fixed costs).

Relevant Range of Operations.   The most likely boundaries of business volume.

Success Determinants.   The internal variables that affect the successful performance of the enterprise.

Variable Cost Ratio.   The result obtained from dividing variable costs by sales.

REFERENCES

Buchele, Robert B. *Business Policy in Small and Growing Firms.* New York: Harper & Row, 1967.

Buskirk, Richard H., and Vaughn, Percy J., Jr. *Managing New Enterprises.* St. Paul, MN: West Publishing Co., 1976.

Clark, Charles T., and Schkade, Lawrence L. *Statistical Analysis for Administrative Decisions.* Cincinnati, OH: South-Western Publishing Co., 1979.

Collins, Orvis, and Moore, David G. *The Organization Makers.* New York: Appleton-Century-Crofts, 1970.

Deeks, John. *The Small Firm Owner-Manager.* New York: Holt, Rinehart & Winston, 1976.

Dible, Donald M. *Up Your Own Organization.* Santa Clara, CA: Entrepreneur Press, 1971.

Findlay, M. Chapman, III, and Williams, Edward E. *An Integrated Analysis for Managerial Finance.* Englewood Cliffs, NJ: Prentice-Hall, Inc., 1970.

Hanan, Mack. *Venture Management.* New York: McGraw-Hill Book Co., 1976.

Hoad, William M., and Rosko, Peter. *Management Factors Contributing To the Success and Failure of New Small Manufacturers.* Ann Arbor, MI: Bureau of Business Research, University of Michigan, 1964.

Liles, Patrick R. *New Business Ventures and the Entrepreneur.* Homewood, IL: Richard D. Irwin, Inc., 1974.

Mancuso, Joseph R. *Fun and Guts, the Entrepreneur's Philosophy.* Reading, MA: Addison Wesley, 1973.

Mayer, Kurt B., and Goldstein, Sidney. *The First Two Years: Problems of Small Firm Growth and Survival.* Washington, DC: Small Business Administration, U.S. Government Printing Office, 1961.

McClelland, David. *The Achieving Society.* Princeton, NJ: Van Nostrand, 1961.

McGuire, Joseph W. *Factors Affecting the Growth of Manufacturing Firms.* Seattle, WA: School of Business, University of Washington, March, 1963.

Schumpeter, Joseph A. *The Theory of Economic Development.* Cambridge, MA: Harvard University Press, 1934.

Swayne, Charles, and Tucker, William. *The Effective Entrepreneur.* Morristown, NJ: General Learning Press, 1973.

Timmons, Jeffry A., Smollen, Leonard E., and Dingee, Alexander L. M., Jr. *New Venture Creation.* Homewood, IL: Richard D. Irwin, Inc., 1977.

Woodruff, A. M., and Alexander, T. G. *Success and Failure in Small Manufacturing.* Pittsburgh, PA: University of Pittsburgh Press, 1958.

Woodworth, Robert T., et al. *The Entrepreneurial Process and the Role of Accountants, Bankers and Lawyers.* Seattle, WA: School of Business, University of Washington, 1969.

4
The Structure of a Complete Plan

Once the planning steps have been accomplished, it is possible to begin preparing the plan itself. It should be remembered that the planning process in general, and writing a business plan in particular, involve a number of iterative procedures that may have to be repeated a number of times before the final plan is ready. Thus, the document itself is the result of conceivably numerous trials and reworkings from the original planning draft. In this chapter, we shall work through an entire iteration of our continuous example (the Jackson Funeral Home) so that all phases of the mechanics of preparation may be illustrated.

THE PLAN OUTLINE

We begin the analysis with the finished product and from this we work back to see how each part of the plan is done. The following is a recommended outline for a complete plan. This is the document that the entrepreneur will use to guide him in actually managing his enterprise. The starred sections of the outline would also appear in the summary (financing) plan that would be presented to bankers, venture capitalists, or other potential investors.

I. Introduction*
   A. A one-paragraph statement about the nature of the business.
   B. A one-paragraph rationale for the existence of the business.
   C. A brief statement about the financing required.
II. Summary of Industry and Venture*
   A. Key characteristics of the industry.
   B. Structure and important features of the company.

III. *Pro Forma* Financial Statements*
  A. Balance sheet at inception.
  B. Income and cash flow *pro forma* statements over the planning horizon.
IV. Complete Analysis of the Industry*
V. Form and Organizational Structure of the Company*
VI. The Strategic Plan
  A. Statement of the enterprise mission.
  B. Definition of the business.
  C. Specific enterprise goals.
  D. Enterprise strategies.
  E. Statement of planning premises.
  F. Strategic long-range plan objectives.
    1. Sales, cost, and profit projections.
    2. Major capital additions (plant, equipment, etc.).
    3. Cash flow and financing.
    4. Personnel requirements.
VII. The Operating Plan
  A. Marketing (sales) plan.
  B. Production plan.
  C. Various expense plans.
  D. Operating income plan.
  E. Cash flow and funds flow plans.
  F. Planned balance sheet.
  G. Planned operating and financial ratios.
VIII. Appendices*
  A. Pertinent contracts.
  B. Technical information.
  C. Other supporting data.

Much of the information called for in the outline will have been developed in the preparation steps already taken (see Chapter 3). For example, the statement about the nature of the business would have been analyzed in Step Two: Definition of the Business; the rationale for the existence of the business should have been addressed in Step Three: Identification of Opportunity; etc.

INTRODUCTION

The introduction should spell out in its first paragraph what the business is all about, who is involved, where it will be located (if that is a relevant concern), and why there is a need for the business to exist. The second paragraph of the introduction should provide a succinct statement about the nature of the business. The third paragraph should describe what financing is required and what will be done with the funds raised. The three paragraphs that comprise the introduction should occupy no more than one page of a typed manuscript.[1]

Ben Jackson has prepared the following introduction for his business plan.

INTRODUCTION TO JACKSON FUNERAL HOME BUSINESS PLAN

The Jackson Funeral Home is being founded by Mr. Ben Jackson to fill the need for an additional funeral service location in Wesson, New Jersey. Presently, Wesson has twelve funeral homes, but there is a demand for another location to serve the increasingly elderly community that lives in the downtown part of the city [see the Report of Market Analysis, Inc. in the Appendix (to this plan)].

Funeral concerns provide two basic services to society: (1) Care of the dead, and (2) assistance to survivors. The means of caring for the dead depends on the customs, laws, and physical environment of a given culture. In the United States, most families employ the services of a funeral director to take charge of the details of providing such care. American funeral practice has evolved over the years to minimize the inconvenience of the living. Thus, the typical funeral home will also seek to assist the family in whatever way it can.

The estimated required investment to begin operations is $160,000. Mr. Jackson will invest $20,000 of his personal funds in the business and $20,000 will be borrowed from a local bank. The balance of $120,000 is solicited from an outside investor or venture capitalist who will lend the company $110,000 and who will acquire one-third of the corporation stock for the remaining $10,000 in equity.

SUMMARY OF INDUSTRY AND VENTURE

The next section of the plan should detail key characteristics of the industry in which the venture will participate (or in which it

---

[1] The exact structure of the plan may vary depending on the nature of the business in question and the preferences of the preparer of the plan. The structure recommended here has been proven successful, however, and the authors feel it is a sound one. Variations on possible plan structures are illustrated in the sample plans in the Appendix to this book.

currently participates) and the venture itself. Two or three paragraphs should be devoted to summarizing the detailed industry analysis which will appear later in the business plan. This summary requires the entrepreneur to focus attention on the salient external variables that will influence his business (see discussion in Chapter 3). Next, key features of the specific venture should be discussed. Two or three paragraphs should be prepared to provide focus on the particular business envisaged and how the entity will be financed.

SUMMARY OF INDUSTRY AND VENTURE FOR THE JACKSON FUNERAL HOME

The most recent U.S. Department of Commerce census data indicate that there are 19,622 funeral home locations in the United States. The majority of these are owned and operated by families who have been in the funeral business for generations. Despite its fragmentation, the funeral service industry is an important economic market. Consumer expenditures on funerals and burials are estimated to exceed $4 billion per year.

The most important determinant of the demand for funerals is the number of deaths which occur in a given market area. For many years, the aggregate mortality rate in the United States has been declining. As demographers look to the 1980s and 1990s, it becomes increasingly obvious that the death rate will rise dramatically as the age distribution of the population shifts in favor of the elderly.

Most funeral businesses are characterized by the existence of high levels of fixed costs and substantial excess capacity. Because of the high fixed cost nature of the business, volume becomes an important consideration in determining funeral home profitability. As a firm becomes larger, and moves to the positive side of its break-even point, small increases in case volume can produce substantial percentage increases in profitability. It is possible to handle 100, 150, or even 200 services for about the same level of fixed costs. Thus, the 200-case-volume firm will be much more profitable than the one doing half that amount of business.

The proposed Jackson Funeral Home plans to take advantage of the demographic trends that will be apparent in Wesson, New Jersey over the next few years. The population of Wesson is becoming increasingly aged, and there will clearly be an increase in the demand for the services of funeral directors as a result. The firm will begin operations with Mr. Ben Jackson and two assistants.

Mr. Jackson is licensed in both New Jersey and New York, and he will have another licensed professional join him in the endeavor. The third employee will be a clerical receptionist who has funeral home experience and can help with family counselling and other matters.

There now exists a funeral home location on Second Avenue in Wesson that was closed with the death of its owner last year. The building is owned by the widow of the former owner who was physically unable to maintain operations of the business. She has been contacted, however, and has agreed to lease the land and building to Jackson Funeral Home, Inc. with a purchase option.

Jackson Funeral Home, Inc. is a corporation chartered in the state of New Jersey. The firm plans to begin business on or about December 1, 1982. Approximately $160,000 will be required. Of this amount, $5,000 will be spent to purchase inventory (approximately 20 caskets @ $250 average cost); $30,000 will be spent on furniture and fixtures and $20,000 on leasehold improvements; another $60,000 will be required for the purchase of vehicles (a limousine, a hearse, and a lead car); and $45,000 will remain for working capital. The firm will be financed as follows:

Bank loan	$ 20,000
Subordinated debt	110,000
Common stock	30,000
	$160,000

Jackson Funeral Home, Inc. seeks to raise $120,000 from an outside investor or venture capitalist. It is proposed that $110,000 of this amount be in the form of a subordinated term credit payable over the next four years, interest only for the first two years, with an interest rate of 16%. The remaining $10,000 will be employed to purchase 33 1/3% of the common stock of the company. Mr. Ben Jackson will invest $20,000 of his personal funds to purchase the other 66 2/3% of the common stock.

PRO FORMA FINANCIAL STATEMENTS

Pro Forma financial statements should follow the summary of the industry and proposed venture. First, a *pro forma* balance sheet should be prepared to reflect the asset and liability position of the enterprise at the day operations commence (or at the beginning of the planning period if the business is already a going concern). The balance sheet should categorize the funds commitment that the firm contemplates (assets) and where the money will come from to finance the endeavor (liabilities).

A *pro forma* income statement and funds flow analysis should also be prepared for each year of the planning period. Detailed projections of revenues, expense items, expected profits, debt service, and funds flow should be made. Footnotes to the statements should be provided to explain the assumptions behind each figure.

Pro forma data result from the planning process. Each number embodies an initial forecast figure which has subsequently been refined depending upon the objectives of the enterprise. The *pro forma* statements are thus based upon the strategic and operating plans that follow in the business plan (see below). It will probably be necessary for the entrepreneur to involve his accountant in preparing both the *pro forma* balance sheet and the *pro forma* statement of income and funds flow.

After preparing his strategic and operating plans, Mr. Ben Jackson and his accountant were able to construct the *pro forma* financial statements shown in Tables 4-1 and 4-2.

Table 4-1
Pro Forma Financial Statements for the Jackson Funeral Home

JACKSON FUNERAL HOME, INC.
PRO FORMA BALANCE SHEET
DECEMBER 1, 1982

Assets		Liabilities	
Cash	$ 45,000	Note payable (1)	$ 20,000
Inventory	5,000	Subordinated debt (2)	110,000
Furniture, fixtures and		Stockholders equity (3)	30,000
equipment	30,000		
Leasehold improvements	20,000		
Vehicles	60,000		
	$160,000		$160,000

See accompanying notes.

Table 4-2
JACKSON FUNERAL HOME, INC.
PRO FORMA INCOME AND FUNDS FLOW
1983-1986

	1983	1984	1985	1986
Revenues (4)	$156,200	$178,200	$211,200	$261,100
Cost of Services (5)				
Merchandise	28,100	32,100	38,000	47,000
Salaries	62,500	71,300	84,500	104,400
Facilities	23,400	26,700	31,700	39,200
Vehicles	18,700	24,900	25,300	10,400
Administrative/ promotion	2,300	1,800	2,100	2,600
Total operating costs	135,000	156,800	181,600	203,600
Operating income	21,200	21,400	29,600	57,500
Interest expense (6)	21,200	21,200	21,200	12,400
Income before taxes	-0-	200	8,400	45,100
Income taxes (7)	-0-	-0-	-0-	-0-
Net income	-0-	200	8,400	45,100
Add: Depreciation (8)	22,500	33,800	32,700	10,500
Deduct: Debt payment	-0-	-0-	55,000	55,000
Net funds flow	22,500	34,000	(13,900)	600
Cumulative NFF	$ 22,500	$ 56,500	$ 42,600	$ 43,200

JACKSON FUNERAL HOME, INC.
NOTES TO PRO FORMA FINANCIAL STATEMENTS

1. The $20,000 Note Payable will be to the Wesson National Bank and will bear interest at a rate of prime plus 2% It is assumed that prime will be at 16% throughout the life of the Note. The Note will be secured by the inventory, furniture, fixtures, and equipment of the Jackson Funeral Home, Inc. Wesson National Bank has agreed to renew the Note on an annual basis over a four-year period and convert it to a revolving line of credit after two years, assuming the financial condition of Jackson Funeral Home, Inc. is satisfactory.

2. The $110,000 Subordinated Note will bear interest at a fixed rate of 16%. The Note will require the payment of interest only for the first two years and will be repaid in two equal installments of $55,000 on Dec. 31, 1985 and Dec. 31, 1986.

3. The shareholders of Jackson Funeral Home, Inc. will be:

Outside investor	$10,000	(33.3%)
Mr. Ben Jackson	20,000	(66.7%)
	$30,000	(100.0%)

4. Revenues are projected as follows:

Year	Number of Adult Services Handled	Average Revenue per Service	Total Adult Service Revenues
1983	93	$1,400	$130,000
1984	99	1,500	148,500
1985	110	1,600	176,000
1986	128	1,700	217,600

The projection of the number of services handled was made by Market Analysis, Inc. (see Chapter 3). Market Analysis also examined median family income levels, consumer price income data, and per service funeral expenditures for Wesson. They found income levels and prices to be somewhat below the national average. As a result, the projected average revenue per service for Jackson is expected to be below the anticipated national experience (see Chapter 3). Other revenues (clothing, flower sales, grave liner sales, etc.) will equal 20% of adult service revenues.

5. Cost of services are calculated as a percentage of total revenue. Standard cost percentages for the industry, as determined by the principal trade association, are as follows:

Merchandise	18%
Salaries	40
Facilities	15
Vehicles	12
Total	85%

These standard cost percentages will be used except for vehicle expense in 1984, where a 14% amount will be used and 1986, where a 4% figure will be used. The use of ACRS (see discussion in Note 8) necessitates employing these numbers.

An administrative/promotion budget will be prepared each year according to perceived requirements. For 1983, $2,300 will be expended on administration and promotion. Thereafter, 1 percent of revenues will be set aside for this purpose.

6. Interest on the $20,000 bank loan will be (18% X $20,000) = $3,600 per year. Interest on the subordinated debt will be:

Year	Balance	Rate	Interest
1983	$110,000	16%	$17,600
1984	110,000	16	17,600
1985	110,000	16	17,600
1986	55,000	16	8,800

7. Federal income taxes are calculated to average 15% of pretax income. However, investment tax credits eliminate any liability over the next four years. Under the Economic Recovery Tax Act of 1981, 3-year class assets have a 6% credit. Vehicles fall into this category. Thus, the credits for the $60,000 investment in vehicles would be: $60,000 X 6% = $3,600. Under the Act, 5-year class assets have the full 10% credit. Furniture, fixtures, equipment, and leasehold improvements fall into this category. Thus, the credits for the $50,000 investment in furniture, fixtures, equipment, and leasehold improvements would be: $50,000 X 10% = $5,000. The total credits of $8,600 exceed the expected tax liability through 1986.

8. The Economic Recovery Tax Act of 1981 provides for classes of 3, 5, 10, and 15 years for tangible property. The 3-year class consists of automobiles, light-duty trucks, and certain other equipment. The vehicles purchased by the Jackson Funeral Home, Inc. have been determined to fall into this class. The 5-year class consists of most other machinery and equipment. The furniture, fixtures, equipment, and leasehold improvements of the Jackson Funeral Home, Inc. have been determined to fall into this class. The Act established a system known as the Accelerated Cost Recovery System (ACRS) for expensing fixed assets. The recovery allowance for 3-year and 5-year class property is given below:

Ownership Year	3-Year Class	5-Year Class
1	25%	15%
2	38	22
3	37	21
4	—	21
5	—	21

Thus, depreciation (capital cost recovery) for the fixed assets of the Jackson Funeral Home, Inc. will be as follows:

Year	Furniture, etc.	Improvements	Vehicles	Total
1983	$4,500	$3,000	$15,000	$22,500
1984	6,600	4,400	22,800	33,800
1985	6,300	4,200	22,200	32,700
1986	6,300	4,200	–	10,500
1987	6,300	4,200	–	10,500

COMPLETE ANALYSIS OF THE INDUSTRY

The next section of the business plan should contain a detailed analysis of the industry in which the proposed venture will operate. The economic, social, demographic, and political characteristics of the industry should be explored in depth.

Data about the industry may be secured from the U.S. Department of Commerce. Almost every business has a standard industrial classification (SIC) code and census data are gathered every five years indicating total industry receipts, number of employees, industry structure, etc. Forecasts and projections are provided for many industries in the Department of Commerce's *U.S. Industrial Outlook* (available at most U.S. Government Bookstores). Industry data may also be secured from trade associations (which exist for practically every industry), from specific studies done by economists and others, and from large firms in the industry. The entrepreneur should do a thorough library research project on the industry which he intends to enter as one of his first steps in starting a new business.

INDUSTRY ANALYSIS: THE FUNERAL HOME BUSINESS[2]

Funeral concerns provide two basic services to society: (1) care of the dead, and (2) assistance to survivors. The first of these prevails universally as a necessary function in all societies. The second has rather uniquely developed in North America.

The means of caring for the dead depends on the customs, laws, and physical environment of a given culture. In the United States, most families employ the services of a funeral director to take charge of the details of disposition. It is generally desired that the remains be transferred from the place of death as soon as possible, and funeral establishments are equipped to accomplish this task quickly and efficiently. The historic custom was to maintain the deceased in the family

---

[2] Adapted from Williams, Edward E. *Service Corporation International: A Decade of Growth and Development*, Houston, TX, 1981.

home during the grieving period (usually from one to several days), but the trend toward urban living with smaller houses and increased apartment dwelling has made this impractical. Today, the usual procedure is to have the dead removed to a funeral home where the body is embalmed, prepared, and placed in state for viewing. After one or more days, a funeral service is held (typically at a church or the funeral home) and the remains are made ready for ultimate disposition. Although all of these services (removal, embalming, preparation, funeral service, conveyance, and disposition) are not used by every family, virtually all deaths result in the utilization of at least some of the services offered by a funeral home.

In the process of caring for the dead, the average funeral home will offer a number of merchandise items including caskets, outside grave liners, vaults, and burial clothing. Some locations also maintain florist shops, and those funeral homes that perform a large number of cremation services may offer a selection of cremation urns. Historically, merchandise played a unique role in the development of the funeral industry, and many modern-day funeral homes have their roots in cabinet and carpentry shops which also manufactured coffins. Nevertheless, in terms of both importance and cost, the casket is currently only one of the many services/products offered by the funeral industry.

American funeral practice has evolved over the years to minimize the inconvenience of the living. Thus, in addition to providing the aforementioned products and services, the typical funeral director will also arrange for conveyance of the remains to distant localities, obtain death certificates, provide statistical reports to public health agencies, prepare newspaper notices, aid in the collection of government benefits, secure the services of other professionals (such as clergymen, policemen, organists) and assist in the notification of relatives.

The most recent U.S. Department of Commerce census data indicate that there are 19,622 funeral home locations in the United States. The majority of these are owned and operated by families who have been in the funeral business for generations. At present there are just over 1,000 multiunit funeral concerns, and only a few of these are publicly held. The largest funeral concern owns just under 2% of the total number of locations and generates slightly more than 4% of aggregate industry revenues. Despite its fragmentation, the funeral service industry is an important economic market. Consumer expenditures on funerals and burials are estimated to be in excess of $4 billion.

Market studies have discovered several significant variables which determine funeral receipts. The more significant ones include: (1) the mortalities in a given market area, (2) median family income in that area, (3) the proportion of inhabitants over age 65, and (4) the proportion of inhabitants of foreign extraction. The first of these is by far the most significant. In fact, demographic factors are of such significance as determinants that a detailed analysis of population trends, life expectancies, and mortality rates must be made in order to appraise the historical performance and future prospects of the industry.

The death rate per thousand population has declined steadily from about 14.7 persons in 1910 to an all-time low of 8.7 in 1979. Nevertheless, in the past the population increased substantially during most periods such that the absolute number of deaths grew from 697,000 in 1910 to 1,906,000 in 1979. During the 1970s, however, a sharp drop in the birth rate slowed the growth of the population. The reduction in the rate of growth of the population, together with a continued drop in the death rate, produced an absolute decline in the number of deaths recorded for several years during the decade. As a result, the number of deaths occurring in 1979 was slightly smaller than in 1970. Needless to say, this condition has had a negative impact on funeral home revenues.

As demographers look to the 1980s and 1990s, it becomes increasingly obvious that the death rate will increase dramatically as the age distribution of the population shifts in favor of the elderly. There are currently about 25 million Americans age 65 or older (11% of the population). By 1990, that figure should approach 30 million (13% of the population). As the Department of Commerce points out, "The death rate, which declined from 9.4 per 1,000 in the early 1970s to 8.8 per 1,000 in 1977 and 1978, is expected to rise by the mid-1980s as today's large senior adult population moves past the age of 75."

Although most Americans have a traditional funeral service at death, the preferred means of final disposition of the body varies by geography and the socioeconomic status of the family of the deceased. Ground interment of the remains is still the choice of most people, but garden crypt or mausoleum entombment is also becoming popular. Cremation prior to final disposition is increasingly favored in certain parts of the United States as well, and approximately 9.4% of all deaths in the United States now result in cremation. Nevertheless, it should be remembered that only a few families elect to have a "direct cremation" without benefit of a funeral ceremony of some type, and the funeral/cemetery industry provides urns, cemetery garden space, and columbarium niches for the ashes of most of those who are cremated.

In March, 1979, the Federal Trade Commission approved in principle a proposed Rule to regulate funeral industry practices. In May, 1980, however, the FTC Improvements Act of 1980 was signed into law. A section of this Act limited the Commission's authority to regulate the funeral industry and stated that, if the Commission elected to issue a funeral Rule, such rule would have to be limited to those provisions restricted by the Act.

Most funeral businesses are characterized by the existence of high levels of fixed costs and substantial excess capacity which must be maintained to meet peak-load periods of demand. Salaries, which for all intents and purposes are a fixed cost for a funeral home, average about 40% of the revenues of American funeral homes. Facilities account for another 15% and vehicles require about 12%. The most important variable cost is merchandise, and this expense item accounts for about 18% of the funeral revenue dollar.

Although the level of fixed costs for the typical funeral operation is high, this does not necessarily imply that funeral homes are subject to substantial business risk. Actually, the contrary is usually true. Cash flows in the industry are stable due to the nature of the business, and bankruptcy is very rare. Funeral homes have a consistent record of suffering the fewest failures of any business in the United States.

FORM AND ORGANIZATIONAL STRUCTURE OF THE COMPANY

The form and organizational structure of the business venture should be outlined in the next section of the plan. This section is useful to the entrepreneur in evaluating his personnel requirements over the planning period, and it is of interest to those financing the business as well. The people in an organization frequently are the most important determinants of its success. For this reason, many bankers and venture capitalists will often provide financing more on the basis of their confidence in the people involved in the deal than on the outlook for the industry or the *pro formas.* Venture ideas are important but they must take specific form and be executed to be worthwhile.[3] Because people play such an important role in the future success of a new (or existing) business, the section of the business plan devoted to organization is also a good place to provide resumes of the principals in the business. A well-written resume frequently will go a long way toward getting the attention of bankers and venture capitalists. Credibility is a key ingredient in getting the confidence of others and a solid resume enhances credibility.

Ben Jackson has determined that he and two other employees will be able to handle the projected volume of the Jackson Funeral Home during 1982-1985. In 1986, another employee will be required to assist in accommodating the expected growth. Ben has prepared an

---

[3] See Ballas, George C., and Hollas, David. "An Idea Ain't Worth a Damn, Unless...," in *The Making of an Entrepreneur,* Chapter 2. Englewood Cliffs, NJ: Prentice-Hall, Inc., 1980, pp. 11-30.

organization chart for the four years in his planning period and has included a resume in his business plan.

Organizational Structure of the Jackson Funeral Home

The Jackson Funeral Home was incorporated under the laws of the State of New Jersey on July 1, 1982. Its organizational structure will be as shown in Figures 4-1 and 4-2.

JACKSON FUNERAL HOME
ORGANIZATION CHART, 1982–1985

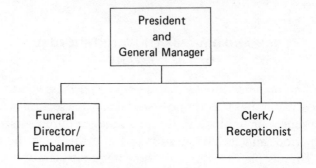

Figure 4-1

JACKSON FUNERAL HOME
ORGANIZATION CHART, 1986

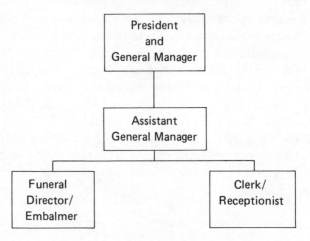

Figure 4-2

Resume

Benjamin R. Jackson, B.S.
Date of Birth: August 21, 1947
Marital Status: Married, one child.
Nationality: American

Present Position
    Since 1978: Funeral Director, Shannon Mortuary, Newark, New
                 Jersey.
    Address: 4875 Gardenia Place
                 Newark, New Jersey

Previous Positions
    1973–1978   Funeral Director and Embalmer, Riverdale Mortuaries,
                various locations in New York and New Jersey.

Education
    1968–1972   New York University, B.S. in Biology
    1973–1974   American School of Mortuary Science

Memberships
                New York Funeral Directors Association
                New Jersey Funeral Directors Association
                National Funeral Directors Association

Church Affiliation
                St. Giles Presbyterian Church

References
                Available on request.

THE STRATEGIC PLAN

Strategic planning is devoted to determining what products or
services the venture is going to offer to which class of customers
in specified geographical areas. The strategic plan is an integral
part of the complete business plan, but it will rarely be included
as part of the summary or financing plan. The strategic plan takes
into account the broad goals of the organization and typically
deals in horizons of several years. The strategic plan emanates
from the steps previously outlined in preparing the business plan
(see Chapter 3). It will contain a statement of the enterprise mission,
a definition of the business, a listing of the goals of the enterprise,

the strategies contemplated to achieve the delineated goals, a statement of the planning premises, and a listing of the specific objectives of the venture over the planning period.

THE STRATEGIC PLAN FOR THE JACKSON FUNERAL HOME

Statement of the Enterprise Mission: To provide the Wesson area community with the highest quality funeral home facilities and services while permitting the proprietor of the business to acheive personal and financial independence and pride in a sensitive service well performed.

Definition of the Business: The Jackson Funeral Home will be a full-service mortuary providing service and merchandise related to the care and disposition of the dead and assistance to their families in the area surrounding Wesson, New Jersey.

Enterprise Goals:
(1) To provide the highest quality funeral home facilities and services.
(2) To be recognized as an honorable and ethical firm.
(3) To provide for the proprietor of the business personal and financial independence and pride in a sensitive service well performed.
(4) To earn a fair rate of return for the investors in the business.

Enterprise Strategies:
(1) To provide a dignified and meaningful service to the people of Wesson.
(2) To price our merchandise and services at a fair and competitive level.
(3) To achieve optimum long-term profitable growth in order to establish a leadership position among Wesson's funeral homes.
(4) To hire and train the most imaginative and competent people available, of high character, principles, and sensitivity.
(5) To develop and maintain an organization whose conduct at all levels and at all times justifies the trust of the community.
(6) To recognize and reward our employees according to their abilities and contributions while maintaining a working environment which makes it unnecessary for our employees to seek outside representation.

Statement of Planning Premises:
(1) We shall be able to lease the location of the old Second Avenue Mortuary and be operating by December 1, 1982.
(2) We shall be able to hire two qualified employees by December 1, 1982.
(3) We shall have opening ceremonies and open house at the funeral home during early December.
(4) We shall advertise our presence during December, January, and February. A special budget will be prepared for this purpose.

(5) The mortality rate in Wesson will stabilize in 1982 while the absolute number of mortalities will decrease slightly in each subsequent year.

(6) We shall achieve a 3% share of the market in 1983 and this will increase to 4% by 1986.

(7) We expect to handle the following number of cases:

1983	93
1984	99
1985	110
1986	128

(8) Income levels will be rising in Wesson throughout the planning period.

(9) Overall inflation will average 9% per year, and we shall be able to increase our average revenue per service by a slightly smaller percentage.

(10) Average revenue per service is calculated to be:

1983	$1,400	
1984	1,500	(7.1% increase)
1985	1,600	(6.7% increase)
1986	1,700	(6.3% increase)

(11) We shall borrow $20,000 from a bank and pay interest averaging 18% on the loan. The loan will be secured by certain assets of the business and will be convertible to a revolving credit.

(12) We shall issue $110,000 in subordinated notes at 16% interest. Such notes will be redeemed in two equal installments of $55,000 on December 31, 1985 and December 31, 1986.

(13) We shall issue $30,000 in common stock.

(14) Other revenues will equal 20% of adult funeral service revenues.

(15) Standard cost percentages shall essentially follow the industry pattern (except for vehicle expense in 1984 and 1986):

Merchandise	18%
Salaries	40
Facilities	15
Vehicles	12
	85%

(16) Equipment will be depreciated according to the accelerated cost recovery system (ACRS) established by the Economic Recovery Tax Act of 1981.

(17) Income taxes will average 15% of pretax income, but the presence of tax credit carry forwards will exceed the expected tax liability through 1986.

Specific Objectives:

(1) Over the planning period (1982–1986), we shall achieve or exceed an annual average rate of growth in revenues of 18%.

(2) Over the planning period, we shall achieve or exceed an annual average rate of growth in operating income of 20% (except for 1984).

(3) We shall achieve the following net margins:

1983	Break even
1984	Slight profit
1985	4.0%
1986	17.0%

(4) Our initial return on total assets (operating income/total assets) will exceed 13% in 1983 and will exceed 30% by 1986.

(5) Our return on stockholder equity (net income/stockholder equity) will exceed 50% by 1986.

(6) There will be no major capital additions during the planning period after the remodeling of the old Second Avenue location is completed in November, 1982.

(7) We shall reinvest in the business the major portions of our earnings and the rest shall be used to reduce indebtedness. No dividends will be paid during the planning period.

(8) No additional financing will be sought during the planning period after the initial $160,000 is raised in 1982. Cash flows from operations shall be sufficient to finance the projected growth.

(9) Our debt/equity ratio shall not exceed 4.5:1 during the planning period.

(10) Our current ratio shall not be less than 2:1 during the planning period.

(11) In 1982, prior to commencing operations, we shall hire a highly competent funeral director/embalmer and a general-purpose clerk/receptionist. During 1986, another employee will be added and the position of assistant general manager will be created.

THE OPERATING PLAN

The operating plan is an important part of the business plan. It determines how to run the venture effectively in the months (year) immediately ahead while progress is made towards the objectives of the strategic plan. The operating plan consists of a marketing (sales) plan, production plan, various expense plans, an operating income plan, cash flow and funds flow plans, a planned balance sheet, a financial plan, and planned operating and financial ratios. Once the operating plan has been determined, various budgets may be prepared to define the anticipated revenue and expense streams. The budgets will become the quantitative statements against which actual performance in the months (year) ahead will be measured.

OPERATING PLAN FOR THE
JACKSON FUNERAL HOME (1983)

Marketing (Sales) Budget

93 services @ $1,400 average	=	$130,200
Other revenue items:		
Grave liner and vault		
sales (50 @ $300)	=	15,000
Clothing (25 @ $150)	=	3,750
Cemetery lot commissions		
(50 @ $125)	=	6,250
Flower sales	=	1,000
		$156,200

Production Budget

The funeral home has one chapel and four staterooms. Maximum capacity is therefore five per day, but an office can be converted into a stateroom if necessary. With 93 services expected, the average expected number of daily services would be:

$$93/365 = 0.25 \text{ per day}$$

Since Sunday services are rare, a more realistic figure is:

$$93/313 = 0.30 \text{ per day}$$

Assuming the average case requires use of the facilities for two days (one day viewing, one day service), we would expect the facility use to be:

$$(2) (93)/365 = 0.50 \text{ per day}$$

These data indicate that at no time should we have to worry about peak-load demand problems. There may be some days when we handle as many as four services per day, and we have the capacity to perform without inconveniencing our client-families.

Merchandise Expense Budget

93 caskets @ $250	=	$23,250
50 liners (vaults) @ $80	=	4,000
Clothing, flowers, and supplies	=	850
		$28,100

Personnel Salaries and Fringes Budget

General Manager	=	$30,000
Funeral Director/ Embalmer	=	20,000
Clerk/receptionist	=	12,500
		$62,500

Overhead Expense Budget (Facilities)

Rent (including insurance, janitorial, and maintenance)	=	$10,000
Depreciation of furniture, fixtures, equipment, and leasehold items	=	7,500
Utilities	=	5,900
		$23,400

Overhead Expense Budget (Vehicles)

Depreciation	=	$15,000
Fuel, repairs, and insurance	=	3,700
		$18,700

Overhead Expense Budget (Administration and Promotion)

Advertising	=	$1,000
Office supplies	=	500
Other	=	800
		$2,300

Operating Income Budget

Revenues	$156,200	(100.0)
Cost of services		
Merchandise	28,100	(18.0)
Salaries	62,500	(40.0)
Facilities	23,400	(15.0)
Vehicles	18,700	(12.0)
Administrative/		
promotion	2,300	(1.5)
	135,000	(86.5)
Operating Income	$ 21,200	(13.5)

Funds Flow Budget

Operating income	$21,200
Interest expense	21,200
Income before taxes	-0-
Income taxes	-0-
Net Income	-0-
Add: Depreciation	22,500
Deduct: Debt payment	-0-
Net cash flow	$22,500

Cash Flow Budget

Cash balance	
(Beginning)	$45,000
Sources of cash:	
Operating income	21,200
Depreciation	22,500
Increase in payables	3,500
Uses of cash:	
Increase in	
receivables	29,000
Increase in	
inventories	1,000
Interest expense	21,200
Cash balance (Ending)	$41,000

Budgeted Balance Sheet

	Dec. 31, 1982	Dec. 31, 1983
Assets		
Cash	$ 45,000	$ 41,000
Receivables	-0-	29,000
Inventory	5,000	6,000
FF&E	30,000	25,500
Leasehold	20,000	17,000
Vehicles	60,000	45,000
	$160,000	$163,500
Liabilities		
Accounts payable	$ -0-	$ 3,500
Note payable	20,000	20,000
Subordinated		
debt	110,000	110,000
Common Stock	30,000	30,000
Retained earnings	-0-	-0-
	$160,000	$163,500

Finance Budget

Assets acquired	
Receivables	$ 29,000
Inventory	$ 1,000
	$ 30,000

Financing Required

None. Internally generated funds (operating income, depreciation flows, and cash) together with
the increase in accounts payable should be sufficient to finance the assets acquired during 1983.

Budgeted Operating and Financial Ratios

Net operating margin $= \dfrac{\text{Operating Income}}{\text{Revenues}} = \dfrac{\$21,200}{\$156,200} = 13.6\%$

Return on total assets $= \dfrac{\text{Operating income}}{\text{Total assets}} = \dfrac{\$21,200}{\$163,500} = 13.0\%$

Return on equity $= \dfrac{\text{Net income}}{\text{Stockholder equity}} = \text{Break even}$

Debt to equity (1982) $= \dfrac{\text{Total debt}}{\text{Stockholder equity}} = \dfrac{\$130,000}{\$30,000} = 4.3 \text{ times}$

Debt to equity (1983) $= \dfrac{\text{Total debt}}{\text{Stockholder equity}} = \dfrac{\$133,500}{\$30,000} = 4.5 \text{ times}$

Current ratio (1982) $= \dfrac{\text{Current assets}}{\text{Current liabilities}} = \dfrac{\$50,000}{\$20,000} = 2.5 \text{ times}$

Current ratio (1983) $= \dfrac{\text{Current assets}}{\text{Current liabilities}} = \dfrac{\$76,000}{\$23,500} = 3.2 \text{ times}$

Receivables turnover (1983) $= \dfrac{\text{Revenues}}{\text{Receivables}} = \dfrac{\$156,200}{\$29,000} = 5.4 \text{ times}$

Average collection Period (1983) $= \dfrac{\text{Days in year}}{\text{Receivables turnover}} = \dfrac{365}{5.4} = 67.6 \text{ days}$

Inventory turnover (1983) $= \dfrac{\text{Cost of merchandise}}{\text{Inventory}} = \dfrac{\$28,100}{\$6,000} = 4.7 \text{ times}$

Average days in inventory (1983) $= \dfrac{\text{Days in year}}{\text{Inventory turnover}} = \dfrac{365}{4.7} = 77.7 \text{ days}$

APPENDICES

The appendices of the business plan should include all pertinent data and documents which add substance to and support the main body of the business plan. Examples of items that may be employed include: contracts, leases, plant or facility layout, major equipment required, other technical information, feasibility studies, market analysis, news stories, etc. Background information on the principals may also be included here instead of in the body of the plan.

APPENDICES FOR THE JACKSON FUNERAL HOME
BUSINESS PLAN

The appendices for the Jackson Funeral Home Business Plan include the Report of Market Analysis, Inc. (see figure 3-1), a copy of the proposed lease on the property (omitted), and the building and grounds plan showing layout of the facilities, parking area, and vehicle circulation (omitted).

SUMMARY AND CONCLUSIONS

The complete business plan will consist of the following: (1) An introduction, (2) a summary of the industry and venture, (3) *pro forma* financial statements, (4) a complete analysis of the industry, (5) a presentation of the form and organizational structure of the company, (6) the strategic plan, (7) the operating plan, and (8) appendices including pertinent contracts, technical information, and supporting data. The summary (financing) plan would be comprised of the same material except for the strategic and operating plans and certain of the appendices.

Once the plans have been prepared, consideration must be given to the methods used for presenting them. Since the complete business plan is subject to change as conditions warrant, it should be compiled in a loose-leaf format in an attractive binder. However, the summary plan may often be in bound form with an aesthetically pleasing cover since it will be given to potential financing and investor sources. It must be a professional-looking volume that will create an immediate favorable impression and cause the reader to devote sufficient time to its analysis.

KEY TERMS

Cash Flow Plan. The cash balance at the beginning of the period plus planned sources of cash (planned operating income and depreciation, planned increases in liabilities, planned decreases in assets) less planned used of cash (planned interest expense, planned taxes, planned dividends, planned decreases in liabilities, and planned increases in assets.)

Complete Analysis of the Industry. A detailed discussion of the economic, social, demographic, and political characteristics of the industry in which the proposed venture will operate.

Financial Plan. An integral part of the strategic and operating plans that determines what assets (inventory, receivables, plant, equipment, etc.) the firm will have to have in order to produce its products (services) and how these assets will be financed (borrowing, earnings retention, sale of stock, etc.).

Form and Organization Structure of the Company. A listing of the key personnel and positions of responsibility in the company.

Funds Flow Plan. Planned operating income plus depreciation, minus interest expenses, income taxes, and debt payments.

Introduction to the Business Plan. A one-page (three-paragraph) discussion of what the business is all about, who is involved, where it will be located, and why there is a need for the business. It should include a succinct statement about the nature of the business, what financing is required, and what will be done with the funds raised.

Marketing Plan. An integral part of the strategic and operating plans that determines what products (services) the enterprise is going to produce, how they are going to be sold, who is going to buy them, and what prices will be charged.

Merchandise Plan. An integral part of the strategic and operating plans that determines what merchandise is to be purchased and sold by the company.

Operating Income Plan. Planned revenue less planned expenses.

Overhead Expense Plans. Integral parts of the strategic and operating plans that identify the overhead requirements for operations. Overhead may include facilities, vehicles, administration, and promotion.

Personnel Plan. An integral part of the strategic and operating plans that determines who is going to make and sell the products (services) of the enterprise, how many people will be required, and what they will be paid.

Production Plan. An integral part of the strategic and operating plans that determines how the products (services) sold by the enterprise are going to be produced, at what cost, in which quantity, at what level of quality, and by what process.

Summary of Industry and Venture. A description of the key characteristics of the industry in which the venture will participate and the venture itself.

REFERENCES

Ballas, George C., and Hollas, David. *The Making of an Entrepreneur.* Englewood Cliffs, NJ: Prentice-Hall, Inc., 1980.

Williams, Edward E. "Innovation, Entrepreneurship, and Brain Functioning." *Frontiers of Entrepreneurship Research.* Wellesley: Babson Center for Entrepreneurial Studies, 1981.

——. *Service Corporation International: A Decade of Growth and Development,* Houston, TX. 1981.

5
Planning and Financing a
Growth Strategy

Thus far in this book we have given consideration to the overall planning process (Chapter 1); we have examined the role of planning in the entrepreneurial function (Chapter 2); we have outlined the steps that must be taken in preparing a business plan (Chapter 3); and we have actually constructed a plan for a prospective new enterprise (Chapter 4). In this chapter, we shall delve more deeply into the mechanics of planning for growth during the first year of operations of a new company (or the forthcoming year for an existing business) and we shall enumerate the means of financing that growth. In the final chapter (Chapter 6), we extend the analysis of planning for and financing growth beyond the first year.

WHAT IS GROWTH ALL ABOUT?

Earlier in this book, we discussed the importance of setting the broad goals and specific objectives of the enterprise as key starting points in the planning process. We stated that any number of possible goals and correlated objectives might be established by the firm and that the principal reason for formally positing goals and objectives was to preclude the pursuit of strategies designed to achieve mutually exclusive (or conflicting) goals. Thus, we maintained that it was perfectly acceptable for an entrepreneur to have public service as his principal goal so long as he recognized that this goal *might* be inconsistent with a second goal of building a highly profitable company. The point of the analysis was that noneconomic goals were quite legitimate and could be incorporated into the business plan. Nevertheless, economic goals normally play an important, if not the most important, role in planning; and virtually every economic goal centers around the concept of growth.

Growth in the First Year

During the first year of operations of the new enterprise, it is critically important to plan for growth on a timely and controlled basis. If revenues do not come in as rapidly as expected, there may be insufficient cash flow to keep the firm alive past the first few months of operations. Alternatively, if revenues grow more rapidly than expected, the business may also run into difficulties as receivable and inventory levels advance beyond the financial capacities of the enterprise. Thus, planning must be even more specific than was done in preparing the strategic and operating sections of the business plan.

For some entities, it will be necessary to construct detailed revenue, production, expense, and cash flow interim budgets by month, by week, or even by day in order to assure the survival of the business. Surprises can kill a fledgling company, and you cannot wait until the end of the first fiscal quarter to find out what is happening. Certain kinds of businesses can get along with monthly budgets and monthly revenue and expense reports. Firms which sell large ticket items infrequently (automobile dealerships, large appliance dealers, builders, etc.) would not get much out of a daily or even a weekly budgeting and control system. A restaurant, on the other hand, might be in deep trouble if management did not plan for and know how many meals were served each day from the very beginning of operations. Businesses which record a number of daily sales where sales may vary rather significantly from one day to the next should prepare daily budgets and daily operating statements. In general, the following budgets should be constructed:

1. A monthly (weekly, daily) marketing (sales) budget.
2. A monthly (weekly, daily) production budget.
3. A monthly (weekly, daily) purchases budget.
4. A monthly (weekly, daily) personnel budget.
5. A monthly (weekly, daily) overhead budget.
6. A monthly (weekly, daily) operating income budget.

7. A monthly (weekly, daily) cash flow budget.
8. A monthly (weekly, daily) funds flow budget.
9. A monthly (weekly, daily) financing budget.

Not all of the above will be needed in every situation, and some businesses will have to have a more detailed breakdown than that outlined. In all instances, of course, the budgets that are prepared within the fiscal year time frame will be based on the operating plan that was included in the complete business plan.

First Year Growth for the Jackson Funeral Home

Ben Jackson has determined that monthly budgeting and control will be best suited for the Jackson Funeral Home. As a result, he has prepared appropriate budgets by month for the first year of operations of his new business. These budgets were based on the operating plan that he prepared and will become a part of a monthly budgeting/control system. That is, Ben will do his budgets by month; he will then have his accountant prepare monthly operating statements at the end of each month. These statements will be used to make managerial decisions about how to operate the business (including a possible decision to cease operations) and will be reflected in replanning to the extent that major assumptions about the business prove to be incorrect. In essence, Ben will employ a simplified version of the management information system flow chart contained in Figure 2-2. The budgets Ben prepared are shown in Tables 5-1 to 5-8.

First, Ben has prepared a marketing (sales) budget that describes the number of funeral services he expects to handle each month for the first year he is in business. He has also estimated the average price he will obtain per service, and he has listed the other sources of revenue he anticipates. The monthly projections reflect what Ben considers to be reasonable expectations about the growth of the firm during the year. Thus, services handled are expected to be few in the early months and to advance in number as the Jackson Funeral Home becomes better known in the community. Ben's figures also are consistent with the seasonal pattern which is characteristic of funeral demand. More people die in the unpleasant winter months than during the summer, and the requirement for funeral services

Table 5-1
Jackson Funeral Home, Inc.
Marketing (Sales) Budget
Fiscal Year 1983, By Month

	Jan.	Feb.	Mar.	Apr.	May	June	July	Aug.	Sept.	Oct.	Nov.	Dec.	Year
Number of services	4	5	7	11	10	10	7	6	6	7	9	11	93
Average price	1,400	1,400	1,400	1,400	1,400	1,400	1,400	1,400	1,400	1,400	1,400	1,400	1,400
Funeral revenue	5,600	7,000	9,800	15,400	14,000	14,000	9,800	8,400	8,400	9,800	12,600	15,400	130,200
Other revenue:													
Liners and vaults	2	3	3	6	5	5	4	3	4	4	5	6	50
Price	300	300	300	300	300	300	300	300	300	300	300	300	300
Revenue	600	900	900	1,800	1,500	1,500	1,200	900	1,200	1,200	1,500	1,800	15,000
Clothing	1	1	2	3	2	3	2	2	2	2	2	3	25
Price	150	150	150	150	150	150	150	150	150	150	150	150	150
Revenue	150	150	300	450	300	450	300	300	300	300	300	450	3,750
Lots	2	3	3	6	5	5	4	3	4	4	5	6	50
Commission	125	125	125	125	125	125	125	125	125	125	125	125	125
Revenue	250	375	375	750	625	625	500	375	500	500	625	750	6,250
Flower sales	40	40	80	120	80	120	80	80	80	80	80	120	1,000
Total revenue	6,640	8,465	11,455	18,520	16,505	16,695	11,880	10,055	10,480	11,880	15,105	18,520	156,200

Table 5-2
Jackson Funeral Home, Inc.
Merchandise Purchases Budget
Fiscal Year 1983, By Month

	Jan.	Feb.	Mar.	Apr.	May	June	July	Aug.	Sept.	Oct.	Nov.	Dec.	Year
Casket inventory (beginning)	20	20	20	20	21	21	22	22	22	22	22	23	20
Caskets purchased	4	5	7	12	10	11	7	6	6	7	10	12	97
Caskets sold	4	5	7	11	10	10	7	6	6	7	9	11	93
Casket inventory (ending)	20	20	20	21	21	22	22	22	22	22	23	24	24
Costs in dollars of caskets purchased (@ 250)	1,000	1,250	1,750	3,000	2,500	2,750	1,750	1,500	1,500	1,750	2,500	3,000	24,250
Cost of caskets sold (@ 250)	1,000	1,250	1,750	2,750	2,500	2,500	1,750	1,500	1,500	1,750	2,250	2,750	23,250
Value of casket inv. (beginning)	5,000	5,000	5,000	5,000	5,250	5,250	5,500	5,500	5,500	5,500	5,500	5,750	5,000
Value of casket inv. (ending)	5,000	5,000	5,000	5,250	5,250	5,500	5,500	5,500	5,500	5,500	5,750	6,000	6,000

Note: Liners, vaults, clothing, and flowers are purchased as required. These items are sold by photograph and no inventories are maintained.

Table 5-3
Jackson Funeral Home, Inc.
Merchandise Expense Budget
Fiscal Year 1983, By Month

	Jan.	Feb.	Mar.	Apr.	May	June	July	Aug.	Sept.	Oct.	Nov.	Dec.	Year
Cost of caskets sold	1,000	1,250	1,750	2,750	2,500	2,500	1,750	1,500	1,500	1,750	2,250	2,750	23,250
Cost of liners and vaults sold	160	240	240	480	400	400	320	240	320	320	400	480	4,000
Cost of clothing sold	30	30	60	90	60	90	60	60	60	60	60	90	750
Cost of flowers sold	4	4	8	12	8	12	8	8	8	8	8	12	100
	1,194	1,524	2,058	3,332	2,968	3,002	2,138	1,808	1,888	2,138	2,718	3,332	28,100

Costs in Dollars

Table 5-4
Jackson Funeral Home, Inc.
Personnel Salaries and Fringes Budget
Fiscal Year 1983, By Month

	Jan.	Feb.	Mar.	Apr.	May	June	July	Aug.	Sept.	Oct.	Nov.	Dec.	Year
General manager	2,500	2,500	2,500	2,500	2,500	2,500	2,500	2,500	2,500	2,500	2,500	2,500	30,000
Funeral director/embalmer	1,500	1,500	1,600	1,600	1,600	1,700	1,700	1,700	1,700	1,800	1,800	1,800	20,000
Clerk/receptionist	900	900	950	950	1,050	1,050	1,050	1,050	1,150	1,150	1,150	1,150	12,500
	4,900	4,900	5,050	5,050	5,150	5,250	5,250	5,250	5,350	5,450	5,450	5,450	62,500

In Dollars

Table 5-5
Jackson Funeral Home, Inc.
Overhead Expense Budget
Fiscal Year 1983, By Month

	Jan.	Feb.	Mar.	Apr.	May	June	July	Aug.	Sept.	Oct.	Nov.	Dec.	Year
Facilities expense:													
Rent	833	833	833	833	833	833	833	833	833	833	833	833	10,000[a]
Depreciation	625	625	625	625	625	625	625	625	625	625	625	625	7,500
Utilities	558	608	608	508	408	408	408	458	458	458	508	512	5,900
	2,016	2,066	2,066	1,966	1,866	1,866	1,866	1,916	1,916	1,916	1,966	1,970	23,400[a]
Vehicles expense:													
Depreciation	1,250	1,250	1,250	1,250	1,250	1,250	1,250	1,250	1,250	1,250	1,250	1,250	15,000
Fuel, repairs, insurance	140	200	280	440	400	400	280	240	240	280	360	440	3,700
	1,390	1,450	1,530	1,690	1,650	1,650	1,530	1,490	1,490	1,530	1,610	1,690	18,700
Administrative/ promotion:													
Advertising	300	200	0	50	50	50	50	50	50	50	50	100	1,000
Office supplies	150	100	0	25	25	25	25	25	25	25	25	50	500
Other	400	225	75	0	0	0	0	0	0	0	0	100	800
	850	525	75	75	75	75	75	75	75	75	75	250	2,300
Total overhead expenses	4,256	4,041	3,671	3,731	3,591	3,591	3,471	3,481	3,481	3,521	3,651	3,910	44,400[a]

[a]Does not add due to rounding.
In Dollars.

Table 5-6
Jackson Funeral Home, Inc.
Operating Income Budget
Fiscal Year 1983, By Month

	Jan.	Feb.	Mar.	Apr.	May	June	July	Aug.	Sept.	Oct.	Nov.	Dec.	Year
Revenues	6,640	8,465	11,455	18,520	16,505	16,695	11,880	10,055	10,480	11,880	15,105	18,520	156,200
Cost of services:													
Merchandise	1,194	1,524	2,058	3,332	2,968	3,002	2,138	1,808	1,888	2,138	2,718	3,332	28,100
Salaries	4,900	4,900	5,050	5,050	5,150	5,250	5,250	5,250	5,350	5,450	5,450	5,450	62,500
Facilities	2,016	2,066	2,066	1,966	1,866	1,866	1,866	1,916	1,916	1,916	1,966	1,970	23,400[a]
Vehicles	1,390	1,450	1,530	1,690	1,650	1,650	1,530	1,490	1,490	1,530	1,610	1,690	18,700
Adm./prom.	850	525	75	75	75	75	75	75	75	75	75	250	2,300
Total operating costs	10,350	10,465	10,779	12,113	11,709	11,843	10,859	10,539	10,719	11,109	11,819	12,692	135,000[a]
Operating income	(3,710)	(2,000)	676	6,407	4,796	4,852	1,021	(484)	(239)	771	3,286	5,828	21,200[a]

[a]Does not add due to rounding.
In Dollars

Table 5-7
Jackson Funeral Home, Inc.
Funds Flow Budget
Fiscal Year 1983, By Month

	Jan.	Feb.	Mar.	Apr.	May	June	July	Aug.	Sept.	Oct.	Nov.	Dec.	Year
Operating income	(3,710)	(2,000)	676	6,407	4,796	4,852	1,021	(484)	(239)	771	3,286	5,828	21,200[a]
Interest expense	0	0	5,300	0	0	5,300	0	0	5,300	0	0	5,300	21,200
Income before taxes	(3,710)	(2,000)	(4,624)	6,407	4,796	(448)	1,021	(484)	(5,539)	771	3,286	528	0[a]
Income taxes	0	0	0	0	0	0	0	0	0	0	0	0	0
Net income	(3,710)	(2,000)	(4,624)	6,407	4,796	(448)	1,021	(484)	(5,539)	771	3,286	528	0[a]
Add: Depreciation	1,875	1,875	1,875	1,875	1,875	1,875	1,875	1,875	1,875	1,875	1,875	1,875	22,500
Less: Debt payment	0	0	0	0	0	0	0	0	0	0	0	0	0
Net funds flow	(1,835)	(125)	(2,749)	8,282	6,671	1,427	2,896	1,391	(3,664)	2,646	5,161	2,403	22,500[a]

[a]Does not add due to rounding.
In Dollars.

Table 5-8
Jackson Funeral Home
Cash Flow Budget
Fiscal Year 1983, By Month

	Jan.	Feb.	Mar.	Apr.	May	June	July	Aug.	Sept.	Oct.	Nov.	Dec.	Year
Cash balance (beginning)	45,000	38,273	30,856	24,115	24,205	26,884	29,819	37,023	44,122	41,966	43,320	44,239	45,000
Sources of cash:													
Operating income	(3,710)	(2,000)	676	6,407	4,796	4,852	1,021	(484)	(239)	771	3,286	5,832	21,200[a]
Depreciation	1,875	1,875	1,875	1,875	1,875	1,875	1,875	1,875	1,875	1,875	1,875	1,875	22,500
Increase in payables	708	208	208	458	208	458	208	208	208	208	208	212	3,500
Debt incurred	0	0	0	0	0	0	0	0	0	0	0	0	0
Stock sold	0	0	0	0	0	0	0	0	0	0	0	0	0
Uses of cash:													
Increase in receivables	5,600	7,500	4,200	8,400	4,200	(1,300)	(4,100)	(5,500)	(1,300)	1,500	4,200	5,600	29,000
Increase in inventories	0	0	0	250	0	250	0	0	0	0	250	250	1,000
Increase in fixed assets	0	0	0	0	0	0	0	0	0	0	0	0	0
Debt repaid	0	0	0	0	0	0	0	0	0	0	0	0	0
Stock redeemed	0	0	0	0	0	0	0	0	0	0	0	0	0
Interest expense	0	0	5,300	0	0	5,300	0	0	5,300	0	0	5,300	21,200
Income taxes paid	0	0	0	0	0	0	0	0	0	0	0	0	0
Dividends paid	0	0	0	0	0	0	0	0	0	0	0	0	0
Cash balance (ending)	38,273	30,856	24,115	24,205	26,884	29,819	37,023	44,122	41,966	43,320	44,239	41,004	41,000[a]

[a]Does not add due to rounding.
In Dollars.

is consequently higher during the months of November, December, January, February, and March than at other times of the year.

Next, Ben has constructed a merchandise purchases budget. To the extent that a firm's inventories are not bought (manufactured) coterminously with its sales, there will be a difference in the purchases and usage of inventory. The inventory purchases budget will be significant in determining the cash flow of the business whereas the inventory actually sold will be employed in determining the operating income of the business. In the case of the Jackson Funeral Home, most of the inventory was bought during December of the previous year (prior to commencing operations) and subsequent purchases coincide fairly well with sales. Notice, however, that Ben has planned for some increase in his inventory levels during the year since he expects to buy 97 units while he only anticipates selling 93.

The merchandise expense budget is determined directly from the merchandise purchases budget. Units sold become expense items in preparing the operating statement.

The next budget prepared by the entrepreneur is the personnel expense budget. For the Jackson Funeral Home this is a rather straightforward matter of listing the employees hired (expected to be hired) and the salaries Ben plans to pay them. Raises, of course, are programmed into the figures. For a more complicated business with hourly workers and other types of incentives than salary, it may be necessary to coordinate a production plan and an inventory plan with the personnel expense plan.[1]

The other expense items anticipated for the Jackson Funeral Home are detailed in the overhead expense budget. Many of these expenses are fixed and are simply allocated by month. It is important to distinguish between fixed *cash* expenses and fixed *noncash* charges, however. Fixed cash expenses (such as rent) must be paid each month and affect the cash position of the company. Fixed noncash charges (such as depreciation) represent items that have already been paid for and are simply being expensed over time in order to provide

---

[1] The reader who has or is planning a manufacturing business or any other type of concern where different product lines and complicated labor requirements are necessary may need a much more sophisticated budgeting system. A very comprehensive set of profit planning budgets is provided in Welsch, G. A. *Budgeting: Profit Planning and Control,* Fourth Ed. Englewood Cliffs, NJ: Prentice-Hall, Inc., 1976.

for an accounting matching of income and expenses. Thus, fixed cash expenses have an impact on the statements of cash (funds) flow whereas fixed noncash charges do not. Both are determinants of operating income, of course.

The next budget prepared for the Jackson Funeral Home is the operating income budget. The operating income budget summarizes the budgets previously discussed and portrays the expected accounting operating income profit anticipated for the business. Notice that Ben Jackson expects to have operating losses during the first two months of operations but that operating income is projected to become positive by March. The firm is expected to continue to have positive operating income until the summer slowdown reduces revenues in August and September. The firm returns to a profitable condition for the rest of the year and is expected to earn $21,200 in operating income for 1983.

The next two budgets are the funds flow budget and the cash flow budget. These budgets will normally be prepared after the operating income budget and describe the movement of cash through the enterprise. The funds flow budget begins with operating income, subtracts interest expense and income taxes, adds back depreciation flows, and then deducts debt payments. It is constructed in such a fashion so as to focus on the ability of the company to service its debt (interest and principal payments). For the Jackson Funeral Home, operating income in 1983 is planned to be just sufficient to cover interest expense. Thus, the firm is expected to have zero net income (i.e., break even) for the year. Of course, no federal or state income tax would be due since the firm does not anticipate having any pretax income. Nevertheless, when depreciation flows are added back to income, the firm is expected to have a positive funds flow of $22,500 for the year. (No debt repayment is scheduled during 1983.)

The cash flow budget begins with the expected opening cash balance from the previous period and then adds in all sources of cash expected. The principal sources include: the operating income for the period, noncash charges that do not affect the cash position but which were subtracted from operating income (the principal noncash charge for most businesses will be depreciation), nonoperating income, increases in liabilities (such as accounts payable and other indebtedness), and the sale of stock. Next, the uses of cash are subtracted. The principal uses are: increases in the assets (besides cash) held by the firm, repayment of debt, redemption of stock, nonoperating expenses (such as interest), income tax payments, and dividend payments. In general, the income generated by the firm plus increases in liabilities are sources of cash while increases in assets (besides cash) and decreases in liabilities are uses of cash. Nonoperating expenses, income tax payments, and dividend distributions are also possible uses of cash.

The cash (funds) flow budgets must be prepared *before* the financial plan can be prepared. To the extent that it appears that the firm will run out of cash during the planning period, it is imperative that financing be sought to restore the cash position. Always remember: A firm ceases to operate when it can no longer pay its bills. Having a positive or negative net worth may have nothing to do with staying in business. Firms with negative worths can oftentimes continue in business for years (hopefully long enough to return to profitability) because they can get enough cash to pay their creditors, while some firms with positive net worths are forced out of business because they run out of cash and cannot liquidate assets fast enough to pay off creditors. Truly it may be said that the survival of a new business depends on its cash flow and not its accounting net income.

The cash (funds) flow budgets for the Jackson Funeral Home suggest that no additional financing (besides a budgeted increase in payables) will be necessary for 1983. Hence, a financial plan is omitted. The cash position opens with the $45,000 remaining from the original financing in 1982 (after the purchase of inventories, furniture, fixtures, equipment, leasehold improvements, and vehicles). The position is expected to deteriorate during the first four months of operations due to low volume, the necessity of extending credit to client families, and the requisite interest on outstanding indebtedness. The position is anticipated to improve gradually over the rest of the year (except for September and December) as volume improvements more than offset the other cash requirements. The company is projected to end the year with almost as much cash as it began with ($41,000 versus $45,000) despite a $29,000 build-up in receivables and the necessity to pay $21,200 in interest. At no time does it appear that the firm might be in danger of running out of cash unless the volume projections fall well short of anticipations.

DETERMINING A GROWTH STRATEGY

Appropriate growth strategies depend upon the goals and objectives that have been established by the enterprise. What may be a realistic growth objective for one firm may be totally inappropriate for another. In order to assess what is feasible, the entrepreneur will have to have examined the external and internal factors that affect his business (see Chapter 3). Once viable growth objectives have been set, however, the planning and control process again becomes critical to the achievement of those objectives.

To some extent, growth strategies depend upon the relative past success of the enterprise. Thus, it is necessary to measure past objectives against actual accomplishments. This is done by considering the budgets (and long range plans) of the enterprise in light of achieved operating results.

Development of a Growth Strategy for the Jackson Funeral Home

Let us suppose that the year 1983 has passed and Ben Jackson has before him the operating statements for that year. As a good manager, he has spent some time comparing the actual results of the year with the budgeted objectives he had prepared the previous year. An analysis of actual with budgeted figures is shown in Tables 5-9 to 5-12.

Table 5-9
Jackson Funeral Home, Inc.
Comparison of Actual vs. Budgeted Revenues
Fiscal Year 1983

	Actual	Budget	Variance
Number of services	86	93	(7)
Average price	$ 1,525	$ 1,400	$ 125
Funeral revenue	131,150	130,200	950
Other revenue:			
Liners	13,045	15,000	(1,955)
Clothing	3,628	3,750	(122)
Lots	5,043	6,250	(1,207)
Flower sales	1,166	1,000	166
Total revenues	$154,032	$156,200	($2,168)

Table 5-10
Jackson Funeral Home, Inc.
Comparison of Actual vs. Budgeted Expenses
Fiscal Year 1983

	Actual	Budget	Variance
Cost of merchandise	$ 27,736	$ 28,100	$ 364
Salaries	62,500	62,500	0
Facilities expense	26,281	23,400	(2,881)
Vehicle expense	20,048	18,700	(1,348)
Administrative, promo- tion	2,740	2,300	(440)
	$139,305	$135,000	($4,305)

Table 5-11
Jackson Funeral Home, Inc.
Comparison of Actual vs. Budgeted Net Income
Fiscal Year 1983

	Actual	Budget	Variance
Revenues	$154,032	$156,200	($2,168)
Expenses	139,305	135,000	(4,305)
Operating income	14,727	21,200	(6,473)
Interest expense	21,200	21,200	0
Income before taxes	(6,473)	0	(6,473)
Income taxes	0	0	0
Net income	$ (6,473)	0	($6,473)

Of course, Ben has been carefully examining his actual operating results each month and has compared them with his budgets. For the first two months of operations, the number of services handled was well below expectation (one in January versus four budgeted, and two in February versus five budgeted). His expenses were somewhat higher than expected, and his cash flow was running substantially negative. As a consequence, Ben spent more than he had originally anticipated on promotion and he did not replenish his casket inventory as sales were made. By March, volume was closer to budget (five services versus seven budgeted) and by April he was exactly on budget. He continued to watch his cash balances carefully, ordering only part of the inventory that had been sold. He also took the

Table 5-12
Jackson Funeral Home, Inc.
Comparison of Actual vs. Budgeted Cash Flow
Fiscal Year 1983

	Actual	Budget	Variance
Cash balance			
(beginning year)	$45,000	$45,000	$ 0
Sources of cash:			
Operating income	14,727	21,200	(6,473)
Depreciation	22,500	22,500	0
Increase in payables	5,350	3,500	1,850
Debt incurred	0	0	0
Stock sold	0	0	0
Uses of Cash:			
Increase in receivables	18,847	29,000	10,153
Increase in inventories	(428)	1,000	1,428
Increase in fixed assets	0	0	0
Debt repaid	0	0	0
Stock redeemed	0	0	0
Interest expense	21,200	21,200	0
Income taxes paid	0	0	0
Dividends paid	0	0	0
Cash balance (ending)	$47,958	$41,000	$ 6,958

maximum payment terms offered to him by suppliers thereby increasing his accounts payable and reducing the immediate demand on his cash. In May, he was actually over budget by one service, while he was two under in June, three under in July, and on budget in August. Volume picked up unexpectedly in September (three over budget) and continued above budget or on budget for the rest of the year. Ben completed fiscal 1983 having handled 87 services, only seven short of his budgeted objective. During the remainder of the year, Ben aggressively collected his accounts receivable, and he was in a positive cash position for the last half of the year.

Upon reflecting on the annual results for 1983, Ben discovered that his shortfall in services handled was more than overcome by the average price he was able to charge per service. Whereas he had expected to make an average sale of $1,400, his actual average was $1,525. Thus, he had a favorable variance of actual over budgeted funeral revenue of $950. Unfortunately, he turned out to have been overly optimistic about his other sources of revenue, and negative variances were experienced for liner sales, clothing, and lot commissions.

His flower sales were somewhat higher than expected, but the overall variance of actual revenues from budget was a negative $2,168. All in all, Ben was not too disappointed by the revenue figures. He had budgeted total revenues at $156,200 and actually had revenues of $154,032.

Ben was not pleased with his ability to keep expenses in line. He was able to sell less expensive merchandise at higher prices than originally anticipated (hence producing a favorable variance in the cost of merchandise), but he was off the mark in facility expenses, vehicle expenses, and administrative and promotion costs. The principal cost categories of error were: utilities (unfavorable variance of $2,881), vehicle fuel (unfavorable variance of $648), vehicle repairs (unfavorable variance of $700), and promotion (unfavorable variance of $440). The latter unfavorable variance was intentionally experienced in order to remedy the volume problem that was suffered early in the year. The total unfavorable variance of all expense categories was $4,305. Thus, given an unfavorable revenue variance of $2,168 and a negative expense variance of $4,305, the Jackson Funeral Home, Inc., had an unfavorable variance in net income of $6,473.

The early months of 1983 were producing substantial losses for the firm and a severe cash drain. As a result of the actions taken by Ben, the cash flow problem was alleviated, and the firm actually ended the year in a stronger cash position than he originally had budgeted. Whereas he had expected to have his cash position go down by $4,000 during the year, it actually improved by $2,958. Stretching his accounts payable (discussed later in this chapter), reducing (rather than increasing) his inventories, and (most dramatically) collecting his accounts in a more expeditious manner than originally expected were the determining factors in causing the cash improvement.

SIMPLE GROWTH CALCULATIONS

In their most elementary form, growth calculations are merely ratios of two (or more) numbers expressed over a time horizon. Thus, if a company enjoyed sales of $5 million in 1981 and $6 million in 1982, it could be said that the firm had a growth rate in sales of ($6 million − $5 million/$5 million) or 20% during that one-year period. A convenient formula may be employed to express the growth relationship:

$$G = \frac{X_1 - X_0}{X_0}$$

where

G = is the growth rate for the period in question

X_1 = is the value of the variable at the end of the period in question

X_0 = is the value of the variable at the beginning of the period in question

The time periods may be years, months, or even days. Longer periods (two years, five years, etc.) can also be considered, and the growth rate may be calculated for variables that are themselves taking place over time (e.g., sales, profits, etc.) or for variables that are recorded at one point in time. For example, we might compare sales from 1981 to 1982 (as in the above illustration) where sales take place *during* 1981 and 1982; or we might consider the volume of inventory as of December 31, 1981, (say $2.5 million) and the volume as of December 31, 1982, (say $3.5 million) and compute the growth rate over the year ($3.5 million - $2.5 million/$2.5 million = 40%).

Growth rates may be determined over periods that have already taken place, but they are also quite useful for planning purposes. Thus, it is often convenient to establish specific objectives that are stated in terms of growth rates rather than absolute numbers. A company may have earned $100,000 in profits for 1982 and its operating plan may call for profits to grow by 20% during the next year. The planned growth in dollar profits would be $(0.20 \times \$100,000) = \$20,000$ and the absolute value of dollar profits would be $[\$100,000 + (0.20 \times \$100,000)] = \$120,000$. The convenient growth relationship formula determined above may be rewritten to solve for the value of the variable at the end of the period in question:

$$X_1 = X_0(1 + G)$$

Thus, one plus the growth rate may be multiplied by the value of the variable at the beginning of the period to get the value at the end of the period. Restating the example, X_1 = ($100,000)(1.20) = $120,000. The derivation of this formula is worked out in the Mathematical Appendix at the end of this chapter.

Although the simple growth formula is fairly elementary, compound growth calculations (to be discussed in Chapter 6) are much more complicated. The reader should understand the mathematics (as well as the arithmetic) behind the two equations above because they are the basis of the more complicated equations associated with compound growth.

Operating Plan and Growth Strategy for the Jackson Funeral Home for 1984

After having reviewed the actual results for fiscal 1983, Ben Jackson has gone back to the four-year plan he prepared before entering business. He sees no reason to change the statement of enterprise mission, definition of the business, the broad enterprise goals, or the enterprise strategies for the Jackson Funeral Home, Inc. based on the results of fiscal 1983. He does feel, however, that the planning premises and specific objectives of the firm may have to be altered somewhat. From the four-year plan, he has iterated the 1983 and 1984 *pro forma* and 1983 actual figures as shown in Table 5-13. He has also listed salient elements of the planning premises and specific objectives of the strategic plan:

Table 5-13
Jackson Funeral Home, Inc.
Pro Forma and Actual Results
1983 and 1984

	Pro Forma 1983	Actual 1983	*Pro Forma* 1984
Revenues	$156,200	$154,032	$178,200
Cost of services			
Merchandise	28,100	27,736	32,100
Salaries	62,500	62,500	71,300
Facilities	23,400	26,281	26,700
Vehicles	18,700	20,048	24,900
Administrative/ promotion	2,300	2,740	1,800
Total operating costs	135,000	139,305	156,800
Operating income	21,200	14,727	21,400
Interest expense	21,200	21,200	21,200
Income before taxes	0	(6,473)	200
Income taxes	0	0	0
Net Income	$ 0	$ (6,473)	$ 200

Premises

1. The mortality rate and absolute number of mortalities in Wesson will stabilize in 1982 and will increase slightly in each subsequent year.
2. We shall achieve a 3% share of the market in 1983 and this will increase to 4% by 1986.
3. We expect to handle 93 cases in 1983, 99 in 1984, 110 in 1985, and 128 in 1986.
4. Income levels will be rising in Wesson throughout the planning period.
5. Average revenue per service is calculated to be $1,400 in 1983, $1,500 in 1984, $1,600 in 1985, and $1,700 in 1986.
6. Other revenue will equal 20% of funeral service revenues.
7. Standard cost percentages shall follow the industry pattern of: merchandise, 18%; salaries, 40%; facilities, 15%; and vehicles, 12%.

Objectives

1. Over the planning period, we shall achieve or exceed an annual average growth rate of revenues of 18%.
2. Over the planning period, we shall achieve or exceed an annual average growth rate of operating income of 20%.
3. We shall achieve the following net margins: 1983, break even; 1984, slight profit; 1985, 4.0%; 1986, 17.0%.
4. Return on assets will exceed 13% in 1983 and will exceed 30% by 1985.
5. Return on stockholder equity will exceed 50% by 1986.
6. There will be no major capital additions during the planning period.
7. No dividends will be paid during the planning period.
8. No additional financing will be sought during the planning period.
9. The firm's debt/equity ratio shall not exceed 4.5:1 during the planning period.
10. The current ratio shall not be less than 2:1 during the planning period.

In reviewing the planning premises, Ben has found that he was essentially correct about the mortality rate and number of mortalities in Wesson for 1982 (see Chapter 3). During the year, there were 3,165 deaths (up from 3,038 in 1981). Preliminary data suggest that the number increased in 1983 to 3,184. Given a population of approximately 308,000 during the year, the death rate was about 10.3 per thousand (up from 9.8 in 1981 and 10.0 in 1982). Unfortunately, the market share for the Jackson Funeral Home was only (86/3184) or 2.7% for the year, somewhat below the 3.0% share premised. Instead of handling 93 cases, only 86 services were provided. On the other hand, income levels did rise in Wesson and average revenue per service exceeded the premised amount ($1,525 versus $1,400). Other revenues fell short of 20% of funeral service revenue ($22,882/$131,150 = 17.4%) and the cost percentages did not follow the industry pattern exactly:

	Industry	Jackson 1983 Actual
Merchandise	18.0%	18.0%
Salaries	40.0	40.6
Facilities	15.0	17.1
Vehicles	12.0	13.0

In considering the achievement of objectives, Ben found it necessary to review the actual and budgeted balance sheets for December 31, 1983. These comparisons are shown in Table 5-14.

Table 5-14

	Actual	Budgeted	Variance
Assets			
Cash	$ 47,958	$ 41,000	$ 6,958
Receivables	18,847	29,000	(10,153)
Inventory	4,572	6,000	(1,428)
FF&E	25,500	25,500	—
Leasehold	17,000	17,000	—
Vehicles	45,000	45,000	—
	$158,877	$163,500	$ (4,623)
Liabilities			
Accounts payable	$ 5,350	$ 3,500	$ 1,850
Note payable	20,000	20,000	—
Subordinated debt	110,000	110,000	—
Common stock	30,000	30,000	—
Retained earnings	(6,473)	0	(6,473)
	$158,877	$163,500	$ (4,623)

From these he determined the following:

	1983 Objective	1983 Actual Result
Revenue growth	Not determined since the firm was not in business in 1982.	—
Operating income growth	Not determined since the firm was not in business in 1982.	—
Net margin	Break even	$\dfrac{-\$6{,}473}{\$154{,}032} = -4.2\%$
Return on assets	13%+	$\dfrac{\$14{,}727}{\$158{,}887} = 9.3\%$
Return on stockholder equity	Break even	$\dfrac{-\$6{,}473}{\$23{,}527^{a}} = -27.5\%$
Capital additions	None	None
Dividends paid	None	None
Debt equity ratio	Not greater than 4.5:1	$\dfrac{\$135{,}350^{b}}{\$23{,}527} = 5.8{:}1$
Current ratio	Not less than 2:1	$\dfrac{\$71{,}377^{c}}{\$25{,}350^{d}} = 2.8{:}1$

[a]$30,000 - $6,473 = $23,527
[b]$5,350 + $20,000 + $110,000 = $135,350
[c]$47,958 + $18,847 + $4,572 = $71,377
[d]$5,350 + $20,000 = $25,350

Thus, Ben failed to achieve many of the objectives he established for himself in 1983. Consequently, he has decided his objectives were unrealistic and that more reasonable objectives will be established for 1984. In light of his original four-year plan and the 1983 operating experience, Ben has assumed the following premises for 1984:

1. The mortality rate and absolute number of mortalities in Wesson will reflect the 1983 pattern. That is, there will be 3,165 deaths. Given a slight contraction in the population, the mortality rate will rise to 10.4 per thousand.
2. Income levels will continue to rise in Wesson.
3. No new funeral establishments will open in the city.

Given the above premises, objectives have been set for 1984. Notice that several of the items that were premises for the first year of operations now fall into the objectives category. This is because a number of variables could only be assumed originally and can only become targets to shoot for *after* reasonable parameters have been discerned. The 1984 objectives for the Jackson Funeral Home, Inc. are:

1. We shall achieve a market share of 3.0%.
2. We shall handle 95 services during the year.
3. Average revenue per service will advance by 5% to $1,600. [$1,600 = $1,525 (1.05)].
4. Funeral service revenue will equal (95)($1,600) or $152,000.
5. Other revenue will equal 17.1% of funeral service revenue (0.171)($152,000) or $126,000.
6. Revenues will grow by over 15% from 1983 to $178,000 ($178,000 – $154,032)/$154,032 = 15.6%.
7. The following cost percentages will be attained:

Merchandise	18.0%
Salaries	40.0
Facilities	16.9
Vehicles	15.7

8. An operating margin of 8.4% will be earned.
9. Return on assets will approach 10.0%.
10. Return on stockholder equity will continue to be negative.
11. There will be no major capital additions or employees hired during the year.
12. No dividends will be paid during the year.
13. No additional financing will be sought during the year.
14. The firm's debt/equity ratio shall not exceed 8:1 during the year.
15. The current ratio shall not be less than 2:1 during the year.

From this set of objectives, a budgeted income statement and balance sheet for fiscal 1984 may be prepared as shown in Tables 5-15 and 5-16.

Table 5-15
Jackson Funeral Home, Inc.
Budgeted Net Income Statement
Fiscal 1984

Revenues	$178,000	(100.0%)
Cost of services		
Merchandise	32,000	(18.0)
Salaries	71,200	(40.0)
Facilities	30,000	(16.9)
Vehicles	28,000	(15.7)
Administration/promotion	1,800	(1.0)
Total operating costs	163,000	(91.6)
Operating income	15,000	(8.4)
Interest expense	21,200	(11.9)
Income before taxes	(6,200)	(-3.5)
Income taxes[a]	0	(0.0)
Net Income	$ (6,200)	(-3.5)

[a]Since the company will have a net loss, no income tax would be due in 1984.

Table 5-16
Jackson Funeral Home, Inc.
Actual and Budgeted Balance Sheets
December 31, 1983 and 1984

	1983 Actual	1984 Budgeted	Change
Assets			
Cash	$ 47,958	$ 60,000	$12,042
Receivables	18,847	30,000	11,153
Inventory	4,572	8,000	3,428
FF&E	25,500	18,900	(6,600)
Leasehold	17,000	12,600	(4,400)
Vehicles	45,000	22,200	(22,800)
	$158,877	$151,700	$(7,177)
Liabilities			
Accounts payable	$ 5,350	$ 4,373	$ (977)
Note payable	20,000	20,000	0
Subordinated debt	110,000	110,000	0
Common stock	30,000	30,000	0
Retained earnings	(6,473)	(12,673)	(6,200)
	$158,877	$151,700	$(7,177)

FINANCING A GROWTH STRATEGY

Once a growth strategy has been determined for the firm for the forthcoming year, it becomes necessary to decide how to finance that growth. Basically, there are two principal types of finance: funds generated internally and funds raised externally. In the finance literature,[2] the distinction is also often made between *gross* sources of finance and *net* sources. Gross internal sources include all the funds available to the firm to finance its operations such as operating income, depreciation flows and other noncash charges, and asset conversions. Net sources are those that remain after depreciating assets are replenished and all payments are made to suppliers of funds and the government. Retained earnings are the principal net source of internal finance since depreciation flows must be used to replenish fixed assets, interest and dividend payments are paid to suppliers of funds, and income taxes are paid to the government.

For the new enterprise, concentrating on net internal sources of finance may be misleading. At this stage of development, the firm is usually fluid and the timing of fixed asset replacement may be more critical than the assumption that fixed assets must be replaced eventually to keep the firm operating (an important reason for focusing on net rather than gross sources of finance). Thus, the new firm may have purchased fixed assets at the founding of the enterprise and those assets may not have to be replaced for several years. In the meanwhile, the depreciation charges that are made for income statement purposes are sources of funds that may keep the company in business. To be sure, if the firm loses money for several years (retained earnings do not become positive), the firm may not be able to replace its operating assets and it may be forced out of business.

Asset conversions are another important source of gross internal finance. An asset conversion takes place when one form of asset is liquidated to employ cash elsewhere or when an asset is liquidated to repay a liability. Technically, depreciation is an asset conversion in that depreciation charges reduce fixed assets and the funds made available may be used to purchase other assets or reduce liabilities,

---

[2] See, for example, Van Horne, J. C. *Financial Management and Policy,* Fourth Ed. Englewood Cliffs, NJ: Prentice-Hall, Inc., 1977; and Weston, J. F., and Brigham, E. F. *Managerial Finance,* Seventh Ed. Hinsdale, IL: Dryden Press, 1981.

but every asset is capable of being converted. Thus, accounts receivable may be collected at a faster rate than new receivables are put on the books. The result is an increase in the cash position of the firm and, hence, the firm has a source of funds that may be used to purchase other assets, pay off liabilities, or even finance an operating loss. Inventories may similarly be worked down at a faster rate than they are replenished. The result is a build-up in cash that may be deployed as necessary. The reader is reminded, or course, that under conditions of growth it is more likely that receivables levels and inventories will be *increasing* rather than declining and will be a *use* of finance rather than a source. Over time, the same may be said of fixed assets. The growing enterprise will probably be adding to its fixed asset base at a more rapid rate than fixed assets are depreciated. Thus, depreciation sources may be insufficient and will not be available to finance other needs.

The firm may also elect to employ externally secured funds. This may be necessary if internal funds are insufficient to finance the growth of the business or simply because funds are available at attractive rates and the entrepreneur elects to substitute external finance for internal. Normally, a distinction is drawn between short-term and long-term means of external finance. Short-term sources include supplier credit, bank finance, and commerical finance and factoring arrangements, among other sources. Long-term finance includes issuance of long-term obligations (bonds), incurring long-term debt (borrowing from intermediaries such as banks and insurance companies), leasing, and selling common and preferred shares. Of course, long-term sources are really long-term in the sense that their repayment takes place more than one year in the future. As a source of cash, however, long-term funds are normally deployed within the year the funds are raised, or, at most, within a couple of years. In this chapter, we shall discuss the short-term sources of external finance, while the long-term sources will be reviewed in Chapter 6.

Short-Term Finance

A principal source of short-term funds may be the firm's suppliers, including some that are not often considered to be sources. For example, to the extent that employees provide useful services to the enterprise prior to the time at which they are paid, they supply funds to the firm at no cost. In addition, a firm earns profits (hopefully) continuously but must only pay taxes quarterly. Within each quarter, the government becomes a free source of funds. The major form of supplier finance, however, is trade credit. Trade credit is granted when a firm purchases raw materials, merchandise, or other items and is not required to pay prior to or at the time of delivery. For example, a supplier may sell on terms "net/10, EOM." This means that payment for purchases made this month are due by the tenth day of the following month. Thus, the supplier is essentially providing funds for at least 10 and conceivably as long as 40 days. These funds are made available at no specific cost, although it may be argued that the supplier includes *his* cost of finance in the selling price for his goods.

Trade credit may also be granted with a discount. For example, terms of "2/10, net 30" mean that if payment is made within 10 days, the purchaser may take a 2% discount, but if the discount is not taken, payment is due in 30 days in any case. The shrewd entrepreneur will pay within 10 days if other, less expensive sources of finance are available. If the discount is not taken, he will take the full 30 days to pay. To do otherwise would involve foregoing an essentially free source of funds. The cost of not taking the discount can be calculated as follows:

$$\frac{\text{Percentage Discount}}{100\% - \text{Percentage Discount}} \times \frac{365}{\text{Total Period} - \text{Discount Period}}$$

In the case of terms "2/10, net 30," the annualized cost of funds would be:

$$\frac{2\%}{98\%} \times \frac{365}{20} = 37.2\%$$

Thus, if an invoice for $960 were presented, only (0.98)($960) = $940.80 would be due if the invoice were paid in 10 days; but $960 would be due in 30 days. The savings, $19.20, is the cost of using $940.80 for 20 additional days. This period of time may be annualized by dividing it into 365, or 365/20 = 18.25. The cost of funds would therefore be:

$$\frac{\$19.20}{\$940.80} \times 18.25 = (0.0204)(18.25) = 37.2\%$$

Although it is recommended that payment be made by the end of the assigned 30-day period, some firms will elect not to do so. This policy is known as "stretching" payables and is followed by weak, cash-deficient companies at most times and by many businesses during periods of tight money. The costs of such a policy in terms of the deterioration of the firm's credit rating, the reluctance of suppliers to sell again on credit, etc., are difficult to quantify but are very real nevertheless. Whenever possible, it is best to apprise suppliers of the problems causing the delay and of when they may expect payment.

Another major source of funds for businesses is bank credit. This is usually the cheapest external form of short-term finance, and the entrepreneur is advised to pay particular attention to developing his banking relationships. Although many firms will wait until the need for financing is imminent before discussing matters with their bankers, good planning procedures suggest that the availability of funds should be ascertained well in advance of need. A well-run business will normally keep some minimum balances in the bank, and this is an important first step toward obtaining a loan. It is also desirable for the entrepreneur to provide his banker with periodic financial statements so that he has a continuing record of the condition of the business. If these two prerequisites are satisfied, the firm should be able to eventually obtain a *line of credit,* which is merely an informal agreement on the part of the bank that, other things being equal, it would be willing to lend the firm up to some given amount at a prescribed interest rate. This rate is normally tied to the *prime rate* (the minimum rate charged to borrowers of the best credit worthiness), such as "prime plus 1%." The borrower may also be required to be out of debt to the bank (or the banking system) for some period during the year to demonstrate his liquidity (the so called "clean-up" provision). Although a line of credit arrangement is useful for the entrepreneur to have, it is not legally binding upon the bank and can be greatly reduced if credit conditions tighten.

If the entrepreneur cannot afford to gamble on having the volume of his borrowings reduced, a more formal credit "revolver" may be arranged. A *revolving credit guarantee* is a binding commitment on the part of the bank to lend up to a given maximum amount at a specified interest charge (usually stated in terms of prime) over a stated period (often a year). As in the case of the line of credit, the bank can extract itself from this commitment if the financial condition of the borrower deteriorates substantially, but it may not dishonor the obligation merely because credit conditions tighten. In return for undertaking the obligation the bank will require that a fee (often 0.5% per year but sometimes a higher figure) be paid on the unborrowed balance. For example, suppose that ABC Company had a $100,000 revolving credit arrangement at prime plus 2%, with 0.5% being paid on the unborrowed balance, and average borrowings of $70,000 over the year. If prime averaged 12% during the period, the total cost of the revolving credit arrangement would be:

$$(\$70,000)(0.14) + (\$30,000)(0.005) = \$9,950$$

Since the average amount borrowed during the year was $70,000, the cost of finance would be:

$$\$9,950/\$70,000 = 14.21\%$$

As we suggested earlier, bankers will examine closely the balances of the entrepreneur who is requesting a loan. There is a greater likelihood that a bank will lend to one of its own depositors than to a nondepositor. A factor in this regard is the feeling of responsibility the bank has toward its depositors, but it should not be ignored that banks make their profits by lending and investing funds deposited with them and therefore wish to reward and encourage the loyalty of their depositors. As a rule of thumb, many bankers feel that their depositors have the right in normal times (assuming the depositor has collateral or is otherwise a good credit) to look to them for loans of four to five times the depositor's normal balance. In return, the banker expects a certain portion of a loan (usually 15–20%) to be left on deposit in the form of a *compensating balance.* The size of this balance will rise during tight money periods when the banker has more bargaining power. The compensating balance requirement will raise the effective cost of the loan to the borrower, but it may be possible to keep the balance in the form of an interest-bearing time deposit (thus cutting the cost of these idle funds) or to arrange for a third party to provide the compensating balance for a fee (a procedure referred to as "link financing"). In the above example, if it were expected that the ABC Company would always have on deposit at least 20% of the outstanding borrowed balance on its revolver, the true cost of finance to the company would be:

$$(\$9,950)/(0.8)(\$70,000) = 17.77\%$$

In essence, the company would have the use of only $(0.8)(\$70,000)$ = \$56,000, and it would pay \$9,950 for the funds.

Bank financing to the new enterprise is frequently not available. Banks are not in the venture capital business, and loans to entrepreneurs are usually made on the basis of the borrowing capacity (personal assets and earning power) of the individual rather than his company. In the case of the incorporated new entity, the entrepreneur will usually have to personally guarantee any loans to his company, and the bank will be looking to the entrepreneur for payment in case the business gets into difficulty.

Banks and commercial finance companies are in the business of making short-term loans on the current assets held by smaller enterprises, and it is frequently possible to borrow from 50 to 80% of the face value of receivables and 30 to 60% of the cost of inventories. If the loan is arranged with a bank, the rate charged may be some 2 to 3% over prime, with an additional fee for handling the receivables of 1 to 2%. If the borrowing is from a commerical finance company, the rate may be appreciably higher. Most entrepreneurs prefer to borrow against their receivables on a "non-notification" basis. Under this procedure, the customer represented by the receivable continues to make his payments to the company, and the company forwards them to the lender. This method is preferred because the customer need not be informed that a third party has been brought into the relationship. It is less favored by lenders, however, because they have less control over the money. On a "notification" basis, the customer makes his payment directly to the lender.

It is also possible to sell (or factor) receivables. This method may have the advantage to the company of shifting the responsibility of credit department costs and bad debt losses to a factoring company if the receivables are sold on a non-recourse basis. Under non-recourse factoring, the factor actually purchases the receivables and has no recourse against the company selling the receivables in the event of non-collection. For this service the factor charges a fee (often around 2% of the receivables purchased) which only covers the credit and collection function. The company selling the receivables must still wait until they are collected before it receives any funds. Should the company want its money sooner, it may obtain an advance from the factor at some stated rate of interest. Should the company keep its money on deposit with the factor after the receivables are collected, it may also receive interest.

Computing the cost of factoring receivables involves taking into account the factor fee, the savings in bad debts generated if the factoring is done without recourse, the savings resulting from not having to maintain a credit department, and the interest paid (or earned) on factored accounts. Suppose the ABC Company had credit sales of $500,000 per year and had an average receivables turnover of five times per year. The average receivable balance maintained by ABC would be $500,000 ÷ 5 or $100,000. If a factor would lend ABC up to 80% of its outstanding receivables at an interest rate of 18%, and charged a fee of 2% on the total volume of receivables factored, the gross cost of factoring would be:

$$(0.02)(\$500,000) + (0.18)(\$80,000) = \$24,400$$

If the company had a typical bad debt write off of $1/2\%$ of sales and would have to spend $5,000 on credit evaluations and collections, its savings would be:

$$(0.005)(\$500,000) + \$5,000 = \$7,500$$

Thus, the net cost of factoring would be: $24,400 – $7,500 = $16,900, or:

$$\$16,900/\$80,000 = 21.13\%$$

It should be remembered, of course, that factoring without recourse means the factor has the right to approve the credit worthiness of the firm's customers. The factor will naturally take a more conservative posture than the company's marketing department might wish, and the result may be lost sales to customers the company would have sold to but of whom the factor would not approve.

Financing Growth for the Jackson Funeral Home for 1984

A review of the 1984 operating plan for the Jackson Funeral Home (see previous section) reveals that no external funds are actually needed for 1984. The only sources of finance will be internally generated. The planned net loss of $6,200 together with depreciation flows of $33,800 will be sufficient to finance the $11,153 increase in receivables and the $3,428 increase in inventory. A planned cash flow statement and projected operating and financial ratios are shown in Tables 5-17 and 5-18.

Table 5-17
Jackson Funeral Home, Inc.
Cash Flow Budget
Fiscal Year 1984

Cash balance, beginning year	$47,958
Sources of cash:	
Operating income	15,000
Depreciation	33,800
Decrease in payables	(977)
Debt incurred	0
Stock sold	0
Uses of cash:	
Increase in receivables	11,153
Increase in inventories	3,428
Increase in fixed assets	0
Debt repaid	0
Stock redeemed	0
Interest expense	21,200
Income taxes paid	0
Dividends paid	0
Cash balance, ending year	$60,000

Table 5-18
Jackson Funeral Home, Inc.
Operating and Financial Ratios
Actual 1983 and Budgeted 1984

	Actual 1983	Budgeted 1984
Net operating margin	$\frac{\$14,727}{\$154,032} = 9.6\%$	$\frac{\$15,000}{\$178,000} = 8.4\%$
Return on total assets	$\frac{\$14,727}{\$158,877} = 9.3\%$	$\frac{\$15,000}{\$151,700} = 9.9\%$
Return on equity	$\frac{-\$6,473}{\$23,527} = -27.5\%$	$\frac{-\$6,200}{\$17,327} = -35.8\%$
Debt to equity	$\frac{\$135,350}{\$23,527} = 5.8 \text{ times}$	$\frac{\$134,373}{\$17,327} = 7.8 \text{ times}$
Current ratio	$\frac{\$71,377}{\$25,350} = 2.8 \text{ times}$	$\frac{\$98,000}{\$24,373} = 4.0 \text{ times}$
Receivables turnover	$\frac{\$154,032}{\$18,847} = 8.2 \text{ times}$	$\frac{\$178,000}{\$30,000} = 5.9 \text{ times}$
Average collection period	$\frac{365}{8.2} = 44.5 \text{ days}$	$\frac{365}{5.9} = 61.9 \text{ days}$
Inventory turnover	$\frac{\$27,736}{\$4,572} = 6.1 \text{ times}$	$\frac{\$32,000}{\$8,000} = 4.0 \text{ times}$
Average days in inventory	$\frac{365}{6.1} = 59.8 \text{ days}$	$\frac{365}{4.0} = 91.3 \text{ days}$

SUMMARY AND CONCLUSIONS

Many businesses fail because the entrepreneur does not engage in the detailed periodic planning and budgeting required to permit the proper evaluation of progress and identification of danger signals before conditions get out of control. Two of the most important financial statements for the new business are the cash flow and funds flow budgets. They must be continuously compared with actual results. Because of the high cost of money in our economy, and the growing tendency to delay in making payments for goods or services received, liquidity (cash flow) is vital to the health of the smaller business.

Throughout this book, the authors have stressed the importance of planning as an anticipatory activity. With careful, realistic, and detailed planning the entrepreneur has greater assurance of success in his venture. The sort of financial planning described in this chapter is a key element in the planning and controlling functions of management. By means of the analysis of actual results and trends as compared with projections, the entrepreneur is in a better position to take advantage of opportunities for increasing profits or to take corrective actions if performance is below standard. This procedure also permits the periodic review and updating of planning goals, objectives, strategies, and premises for the enterprise, thus leading to the development of a continuing growth plan.

Finally, in this chapter we have discussed the sources of short-term finance available to the business owner: supplier finance or trade credit, bank credit, asset-based lending, and factoring. A point to be emphasized is the importance of establishing and maintaining excellent relations with suppliers, bankers, and other providers of finance on a continuing basis. Such relationships, especially with bankers, depend upon the lenders evaluation of a person's integrity, experience, industriousness, and demonstrated ability to control and manage his business.

KEY TERMS

Asset Conversions. Sources of gross internal finance resulting when one form of asset is liquidated to employ elsewhere or when an asset is liquidated to repay a liability.

Clean-up Provision. A requirement that a borrower be out of debt to a given bank (or the banking system) for some period during the year.

Compensating Balance. A portion of a loan which remains on deposit with the lending institution in order to "compensate" for the loan being made.

Externally Generated Finance. Financing secured from sources outside the firm.

Gross Sources of Finance. All the funds available to the firm to finance its operations including all external and internal sources.

Growth Strategies. Plans and policies adopted by the enterprise to achieve stated goals and objectives regarding the ratios of financial numbers expressed over a time horizon.

Interim Budgets. Detailed revenue, production, expense, and cash flow budgets prepared by month, by week, or even by day.

Internally Generated Finance. Funds made available from operations of the business. Gross internal sources include operating income, depreciation flows and other noncash charges, and asset conversions. Net sources are those remaining after depreciating assets are replenished and all payments are made to suppliers of funds and the government.

Line of Credit. An informal agreement on the part of a bank that, other things being equal, it would be willing to lend to a customer some given amount at a prescribed rate of interest.

Link Financing. A procedure whereby a borrower arranges with a third party (for a fee) to provide a compensating balance to a bank.

Long-Term Sources of Finance. Sources that are repaid over a period of time exceeding one year in the future.

Net Sources of Finance. All the funds available to the firm to finance its operation including all external and internal sources less funds required to replenish depreciating assets and pay suppliers of funds and the government.

Non-Notification Receivables Loan. A loan against receivables where the customer represented by the receivable continues to make payment to the company and forwards them to the lender.

Nonrecourse Factoring. A source of short-term finance where receivables are sold to an institution (called a factoring company, or factor) at a discount. In the event of noncollection, the factoring company would have no recourse against the selling company.

Notification Receivables Loan. A loan against receivables where the customer represented by the receivable is notified to make payment directly to the lender.

Payables Stretching. Making payment beyond the term granted by the supplier.

Prime Rate. The minimum rate charged to borrowers of the best credit worthiness.

Recourse Factoring. A factoring arrangement where the factoring company can recover from the selling company in the event of noncollection.

Revolving Credit Guarantee. A binding commitment on the part of a bank to lend up to a given maximum amount at a specified interest charge over a stated period.

Short-Term Sources of Finance. Sources that are repaid over a period of time of less than one year in the future.

Simple Growth Calculations. Ratios of two (or more) numbers expressed over a time horizon.

Supplier Credit. Funds provided when suppliers make available goods (or services) to the firm before payment is required.

Trade Credit. Funds provided when a firm purchases raw materials, merchandise, or other items and is not required to pay prior to or at the time of delivery.

Variances. The difference between actual results and budgeted objectives.

REFERENCES

Findlay, III, M. Chapman, and Williams, Edward E. *An Integrated Analysis for Managerial Finance.* Englewood Cliffs, NJ: Prentice-Hall, Inc., 1970.

Van Horne, J. C. *Financial Management and Policy.* Fourth Ed. Englewood Cliffs, NJ: Prentice-Hall, Inc., 1977.

Welsch, G. A. *Budgeting: Profit Planning and Control.* Fourth Ed. Englewood Cliffs, NJ: Prentice-Hall, Inc., 1976.

Weston, J. F., and Brigham E. F.: *Managerial Finance,* Seventh Ed. Hindsdale, IL: Dryden Press, 1981.

MATHEMATICAL APPENDIX TO CHAPTER 5

We may determine the value of a variable at the *end* of a period by reconsidering the simple growth formula:

$$G = \frac{X_1 - X_0}{X_0}$$

Cross-multiplying, we find:

$$G \cdot X_0 = X_1 - X_0$$

Adding X_0 to both sides of the equation, we see:

$$G \cdot X_0 + X_0 = X_1 - X_0 + X_0$$

or

$$G \cdot X_0 + X_0 = X_1$$

X_0 may be factored out of both terms in the left side of the expression, so that:

$$X_0(G + 1) = X_1$$

and the formula may be rewritten as:

$$X_1 = X_0 (1 + G)$$

6
Planning for Growth
Beyond the First Year

In this final chapter of *Business Planning for the Entrepreneur,* we extend the analysis of the first five chapters and examine planning for and financing growth beyond the first year of operations. In the process, we return to the original strategic business plan that was constructed in Chapter 4 and the revised operating plan that was prepared in Chapter 5. We shall assume that the new business has had one year of operating experience and that the growth to be planned for and financed has taken that experience into account. For the established business, the points covered may be considered to be an iteration of a procedure that should be followed on a regular (probably annual) basis.

WHY GROW?

As the entrepreneur reconsiders his long range goals and objectives after his first year in business, it is wise to reflect on the role that growth should play in his deliberations. There is no law that requires a business to grow. Its sales do not have to advance each year, profits are not required to expand, and margins do not have to be improved year-by-year. Indeed, some entrepreneurs do not wish to have their companies grow beyond a certain size because of the managerial (and other) problems that accompany "big business." On the other hand, it should be remembered that there is a human desire for progress and change. Most of us get bored from doing the same thing year after year, and growth and change do seem to go together. Often it is the case that our most worthy employees are motivated by the stimulation and rewards (financial and otherwise) that accompany a growth situation, and the "brightest and the best" may move on to new associations if they find their current ones to be moribund. Also, there is some truth to the old adage that it may be necessary to grow in order to survive. Without forward momentum, an organization can become lethargic and stagnate in ways other than financial. Thus, it is wise to weigh your growth strategy carefully.

Growing can be risky. A mistake in a larger entity is usually more expensive than when one is made by a smaller organization, although a larger company may be better able to absorb a mistake than a smaller one. As a firm becomes larger, it may be necessary to bring other partners into the operation. Creditors, bankers, and even other holders of stock may become integral to financing growth. The entrepreneur may lose control of his business eventually as it grows to a complex entity. The entrepreneurial skills that so masterfully got the business off the ground and allowed it to survive may not be so necessary to the complicated managerial organization. It might, in fact, be true that the entrepreneur at some point becomes absolutely detrimental to his own business and has to step aside and appoint "professional managers" to run the firm. For many entrepreneurs, this is a stiff price to pay for growth. Alternatively, it may be more enticing to own 15% of a large, publicly-held corporation with stock worth many millions of dollars than to own all of a small business that is illiquid and can, at best, pay its proprietor a good salary.

As the reader may have discovered, this book is not intended to set his goals for him, and now is not the time for the authors to begin to do so. A strategy that has been successful for many entrepreneurs, however, is one that adopts a conservative growth posture. That is, the firm is encouraged to grow as conditions, financing, and opportunities permit. Growth for its own sake is avoided as a strategy.

Growth Calculations Beyond the First Year

In the previous chapter, the simplest growth calculations were made. These were merely ratios of two (or more) numbers expressed over a time horizon. Most readers probably felt the formulas given in the chapter (and derived in the Mathematical Appendix) were intuitively obvious. Nevertheless, growth computations beyond the one-period case are somewhat more complicated and require the use of the simpler equations as a foundation. Computations involving more than one period are done on what is called a *compounded* basis. Thus, if a firm had $100,000 in profits in 1982 and wished to have profits grow by 20% per year for the next five years, the planned profit for 1987 would be:

$$X_{1983} = (\$100,000)(1.20) = \$120,000$$
$$X_{1984} = (\$120,000)(1.20) = \$144,000$$
$$X_{1985} = (\$144,000)(1.20) = \$172,800$$
$$X_{1986} = (\$172,800)(1.20) = \$207,360$$
$$X_{1987} = (\$207,360)(1.20) = \$248,832$$

Notice that all we have done here is iterate the simple growth relationship:

$$X_1 = X_0(1 + G)$$

several times. This can become a nuisance, and, fortunately, a much easier procedure is available. This procedure is based on a rearrangement of the simple formula as follows:[1]

$$X_n = X_0(1 + G)^n$$

Thus, in the numerical example given above, we could compute the profit objective after the first year as:

$$X_1 = X_0(1 + G)^1$$

$$X_{1983} = (\$100,000)(1 + 0.20)^1 = (\$100,000)(1.2) = \$120,000$$

and the objective after the second year as:

$$X_2 = X_0(1 + G)^2$$

---

[1] See proof in the Mathematical Appendix to Chapter 6.

$$X_{1984} = (\$100,000)(1 + 0.20)^2 = (\$100,000)(1.44) = \$144,000$$

By analogy, the following may be determined:

$$X_3 = X_0(1 + G)^3$$
$$X_4 = X_0(1 + G)^4$$
$$X_5 = X_0(1 + G)^5$$

or, in general:

$$X_n = X_0(1 + G)^n$$

For the example above after 5 years, we would find:

$$X_{1987} = (\$100,000)(1 + 0.20)^5 = (\$100,000)(2.48832) = \$248,832$$

Lest you recoil in horror at, say, the prospect of having to compute the twentieth power of a number in order to arrive at a planned sum 20 years hence, it should be noted that these computations have already been made in the form of a compound growth table. This table is presented in Figure 6-1. Thus, if we wished to know the planned profit for 1987 (5 years hence), if this year's (1982) profit was $100,000, and if our objective was a 20% compounded annual rate of growth, we could immediately determine such by examining the table under the 5 year row and the 20% column. The growth factor would be 2.488 (rounded), and the planned profit would be:

$$X_{1987} = (\$100,000)(2.488) = \$248,800$$

The table of compound growth contained in Figure 6-1 may be used for periods and growth rates that are not specifically given, by means of interpolation. Thus, if a firm had sales this year of $250,000 and wished to have them grow at a 13% rate of growth for the next 4 years, we could calculate as follows:

Growth at 12%

$$(1.574)(\$250,000) = \$393,500$$

Year	1%	2%	3%	4%	5%	6%	7%	8%	9%
1	1.010	1.020	1.030	1.040	1.050	1.060	1.070	1.080	1.090
2	1.020	1.040	1.061	1.082	1.102	1.124	1.145	1.166	1.188
3	1.030	1.061	1.093	1.125	1.158	1.191	1.225	1.260	1.295
4	1.041	1.082	1.126	1.170	1.216	1.262	1.311	1.360	1.412
5	1.051	1.104	1.159	1.217	1.276	1.338	1.403	1.469	1.539
6	1.062	1.126	1.194	1.265	1.340	1.419	1.501	1.587	1.677
7	1.072	1.149	1.230	1.316	1.407	1.504	1.606	1.714	1.828
8	1.088	1.172	1.267	1.369	1.477	1.594	1.718	1.851	1.993
9	1.094	1.195	1.305	1.423	1.551	1.689	1.838	1.999	2.172
10	1.105	1.219	1.344	1.480	1.629	1.791	1.967	2.159	2.367
11	1.116	1.243	1.384	1.539	1.710	1.898	2.105	2.332	2.580
12	1.127	1.268	1.426	1.601	1.796	2.012	2.252	2.518	2.813
13	1.138	1.294	1.469	1.665	1.886	2.133	2.410	2.720	3.066
14	1.149	1.319	1.513	1.732	1.980	2.261	2.579	2.937	3.342
15	1.161	1.346	1.558	1.801	2.079	2.397	2.759	3.172	3.642
16	1.173	1.373	1.605	1.873	2.183	2.540	2.952	3.426	3.970
17	1.184	1.400	1.653	1.948	2.292	2.693	3.159	3.700	4.328
18	1.196	1.438	1.702	2.026	2.407	2.854	3.380	3.996	4.717
19	1.208	1.457	1.754	2.107	2.527	3.026	3.617	4.316	5.142
20	1.220	1.486	1.806	2.191	2.653	3.027	3.870	4.661	5.604

Figure 6-1. Table of Compound Growth

Growth at 14%

$$(1.689)(\$250,000) = \$422,250$$

Growth at 13%

Since this is immediately between the two given growth rates, the value would be:[2]

$$[(1.574 + 1.689)/(2)] [\$250,000] = (1.6315)(\$250,000) = \$407,875$$

The table of compound growth may also be used to determine growth rates when two amounts and a period of time are given. Suppose the ABC Co. sold 150,000 widgets in 1982 and wished to sell 300,000 in 1987 (5 years hence). In this case, we would have to solve for the factor that would complete the equation:

$$X_{1987} = X_{1982}(1 + ?)^5$$
$$300,000 = 150,000(1 + ?)^5$$
$$300,000/150,000 = (1 + ?)^5$$
$$2.000 = (1 + ?)^5$$

Year	10%	12%	14%	15%	20%	25%	30%	40%	50%
1	1.100	1.120	1.140	1.150	1.200	1.250	1.300	1.400	1.500
2	1.210	1.254	1.300	1.322	1.440	1.563	1.690	1.960	2.250
3	1.331	1.405	1.482	1.521	1.728	1.953	2.197	2.744	3.375
4	1.464	1.574	1.689	1.749	2.074	2.441	2.856	3.842	5.062
5	1.611	1.762	1.925	2.011	2.488	3.052	3.713	5.378	7.594
6	1.772	1.974	2.195	2.313	2.986	3.815	4.827	7.530	11.391
7	1.949	2.211	2.502	2.660	3.583	4.768	6.275	10.541	17.086
8	2.144	2.476	2.853	3.059	4.300	5.960	8.157	14.758	25.629
9	2.358	2.773	3.252	3.518	5.160	7.451	10.604	20.661	38.443
10	2.594	3.106	3.707	4.046	6.192	9.313	13.786	28.925	57.665
11	2.853	3.479	4.226	4.652	7.430	11.642	17.922	40.496	86.498
12	3.138	3.896	4.818	5.350	8.916	14.552	23.298	56.694	129.746
13	3.452	4.363	5.492	6.153	10.699	18.190	30.288	79.372	194.619
14	3.797	4.887	6.261	7.076	12.839	22.737	39.374	111.120	291.929
15	4.177	5.474	7.138	8.137	15.407	28.422	51.186	155.568	437.894
16	4.595	6.130	8.137	9.358	18.488	35.527	66.542	217.795	656.840
17	5.054	6.866	9.276	10.761	22.186	44.409	86.504	304.914	985.260
18	5.560	7.690	10.575	12.375	26.623	55.511	112.455	426.879	1477.900
19	6.116	8.613	12.056	14.232	31.948	69.389	146.192	597.630	2216.800
20	6.728	9.646	13.743	16.367	38.338	86.736	190.050	836.683	3325.300

Figure 6-1 Table of Compound Growth (continued)

Hence, we are looking for a factor of 2.000 in the five-year row. Scanning across the row, we find the 15% column with a factor of 2.011. This is close enough to say that the ABC Co. is planning for a 15% compounded annual growth rate in the sale of widgets over the next five years. Of course, it may be necessary to interpolate when the numbers do not closely match.[3]

---

[2] This assumes linearity between the growth rates, which is not quite correct. The actual factor for 13% is 1.6304, but the difference is small enough to ignore. For long periods of time at high growth rates, the error can be considerable, however. For example, the factor for 20 years at 40% is 836.683, and the factor for 20 years at 50% is 3,325.300. Interpolating for 45% would yield: (836.683 + 3,325.300)/2 = 2,080.9915. The actual growth factor for 20 years at 45% is 1,687.9518. Nevertheless, it is rare for rapid growth for long periods of time to take place. For example, if a firm had sales of $1,000,000 this year and wished to have them grow by 50% compounded annually for 20 years, the result would be: ($1,000,000)(3,325.300) = $3.3 *billion,* perhaps an unrealistic expectation!

---

[3] Calculators are now available that will easily compute the growth of a variable, given a growth rate, and the rate itself, given two values. For most computations, however, a $5 model that will multiply and divide (and the growth table) will suffice.

Table 6-1
Jackson Funeral Home, Inc.
Strategic Plan 1983–1986
and Actual 1983
Income and Cash Flow Analysis

	1983 (Planned)	1983 (Actual)	1984	1985	1986
Revenues	$156,200	$154,032	$178,200	$211,200	$261,100
Cost of services:					
Merchandise	28,100	27,736	32,100	38,000	47,000
Salaries	62,500	62,500	71,300	84,500	104,400
Faculties	23,400	26,281	26,700	31,700	39,200
Vehicles	18,700	20,048	24,900	25,300	10,400
Adm./prom.	2,300	2,740	1,800	2,100	2,600
Total operating costs	135,000	139,305	156,800	181,600	203,600
Operating income	21,200	14,727	21,400	29,600	57,500
Interest expense	21,200	21,200	21,200	21,200	12,400
Income before taxes	0	(6,473)	200	8,400	45,100
Income taxes	0	0	0	0	0
Net income	0	(6,473)	200	8,400	45,100
Add: Depreciation	22,500	22,500	33,800	32,700	10,500
Deduct: Debt payment	0	0	0	55,000	55,000
Net funds flow	22,500	16,027	34,000	(13,900)	600
Cumulative NFF	$ 22,500	$ 16,027	$ 56,500	$ 42,600	$ 43,200

Growth for the Jackson Funeral Home Beyond the First Year

Ben Jackson has reviewed his four-year strategic plan in light of the operating experience of the Jackson Funeral Home during 1983. The original plan and actual 1983 results were as shown in Table 6-1.

Ben has also taken the revised operating plan for 1984 and attempted to reconstruct a new four-year plan through 1987. Key revenue objectives have been altered to the following:

Year	Number of Services	Average Revenue per Service	Total Funeral Service Revenue
1984	95	$1,600	$152,000
1985	99	1,700	168,300
1986	110	1,800	198,000
1987	128	1,900	243,200

Ben has targeted other revenue at 17.1% of funeral service revenue for 1984, and 20.0% thereafter, and expenses to correspond to the following:

Year	Cost of Merchandise	Cost of Facilities	Cost of Vehicles	Cost of Salaries	Cost of Adm./Prom.
1984	18.0	16.9	15.7	40.0	1.0
1985	18.0	14.9	13.9	40.0	1.0
1986	18.0	13.0	3.4	40.0	1.0
1987	18.0	11.0	3.4	40.0	1.0

Thus, by 1987, Ben hopes to achieve expense ratios superior to those of the industry as a whole.

Given the above objectives, Ben has calculated a new strategic plan for income and funds flow for the next four years, as shown in Table 6-2.

Table 6-2
Jackson Funeral Home, Inc.
Strategic Plan 1983–1987
Income and Funds Flow Analysis

	1984	1985	1986	1987
Revenues	$178,000	$202,000	$237,600	$291,800
Cost of services				
Merchandise	32,000	36,400	42,800	52,500
Salaries	71,200	80,800	95,000	116,700
Facilities	30,000	30,000	31,000	32,000
Vehicles	28,000	28,000	8,000	9,900
Adm./prom.	1,800	2,000	2,400	2,900
Total operating costs	163,000	177,200	179,200	214,000
Operating income	15,000	24,800	58,400	77,800
Interest expense	21,200	21,200	12,400	3,600
Income before taxes	(6,200)	3,600	46,000	74,200
Income taxes	0	0	0	12,800
Net income	(6,200)	3,600	46,000	61,400
Add: Depreciation	33,800	32,700	10,500	10,500
Deduct: Debt payment	0	55,000	55,000	20,000
Net funds flow	33,800	(18,700)	1,500	51,900
Cumulative NFF	$ 33,800	$ 15,100	$ 16,600	$ 68,500

Ben has noted the important role played by depreciation in his plan. After 1985, all vehicles purchased in 1982 have been completely written off. Thus, vehicle expense declines substantially for 1986 and 1987. Ben recognizes that new equipment will have to be purchased eventually and that vehicle expense will rise accordingly at some future point. Ben is also aware of the fact that his cost of facilities will likely rise as well when the current lease expires. Finally, Ben understands that the tax position of the Jackson Funeral Home, Inc. will become less favorable as its income rises. No taxes were anticipated for 1986 despite having planned earnings of $46,000. This was due to cumulative net operating losses (NOLs) of $6,473 in 1983 and $6,200 expected for 1984. NOLs may be carried forward 15 years, and Ben's NOL carryforward expected for 1986 would be:

Year	Income (Loss)	NOL Carryforward
1983	($6,473)	($6,473)
1984	($6,200)	($12,673)
1985	$3,600	($9,073)

Thus, taxable income for the Jackson Funeral Home would be: $46,000 - $9,073 = $36,927. The tax on this amount would be:[4]

Taxable Income	Rate %	Tax
$25,000	15	$3,750
11,927	18	2,147
$36,927		$5,897

Nevertheless, Ben got tax credits of 10% of the value of furniture, fixtures, equipment, and leasehold improvements he made in 1982 and 6% of the value of the vehicles he purchased.[5] Thus, the Jackson Funeral Home, Inc. had 10% × $50,000 = $5,000 plus 6%

---

[4] Under the Economic Recovery Act of 1981, corporate tax rates became:

Taxable Income	Rate (%)
$0 – $25,000	15
$25,000 – $50,000	18
$50,000 – $75,000	30
$75,000 – $100,000	40
over $100,000	46

[5] Under the Economic Recovery Act of 1981, 3-year class assets receive a 6% ITC (investment tax credit) while all other assets receive the full 10% credit. Also, credits may be carried forward 15 years. See previous discussion on p. 65.

X \$60,000 = \$3,600, or \$8,600 in credits to carryforward to 1986. With only \$5,879 due in anticipated taxes, Ben would still have a carryforward into 1987 of \$8,600 - \$5,897 = \$2,703. Taxes expected for 1987 would be calculated as follows:

Taxable Income	Rate (%)	Tax	Credits	Net Due
\$25,000	15	\$ 3,750		
25,000	18	4,500		
24,200	30	7,260		
\$74,200		\$15,510	\$2,703	\$12,807

DETERMINANTS OF GROWTH AND RETURN ON INVESTMENT

Each entrepreneur has his own reasons for wanting to grow and his own strategy for achieving growth. Similarly, each firm has its own peculiar set of growth determinants. No two companies are exactly alike, and the factors that will enable one firm to thrive are not necessarily the same for another — even one in the same general line of business. Nevertheless, there are broad determinants that will be important for many firms. Many of the external variables that were identified in Chapter 3 will be important in determining revenue growth. Overall economic activity, housing starts, consumer expenditures, business investment, interest rates, the rate of inflation, etc., may all be salient factors. Also, key internal variables (identified in Chapter 3 as well) may be relevant. The firm's marketing strategy, its promotion policies, how it prices its products, and its methods of distribution may be quite significant determinants of the revenue growth pattern.

Many of the factors that influence sales growth trends will also influence profit growth. Indeed, it is usually the case that the most important reason for higher profits is a larger sales volume. Of course, the other side of the profit equation includes costs, and expense control can also contribute to growth in net income. Even with a constant or declining sales volume, profits can increase if cost of goods sold, selling expenses, administrative expenses, and other costs of doing business can be brought down.

Growth in return on investment (ROI) will depend on revenue and profit growth plus the investment required to generate increased sales. As a rule, a firm must acquire assets in order to produce a product or service. The asset investment may be in fixed assets (property, plant, equipment, etc.) but the dollars tied up in current assets should not be ignored. For many enterprises, the investment in receivables, inventories, and even cash itself may be a very significant ROI determinant. Just as revenue growth is usually the most important explanation for profit growth, profit growth is typically the most significant factor in improving ROI. Nevertheless, it is possible for a firm to increase its return on investment even when profits are declining if it can reduce the volume of assets required to generate sales.

For many years students of finance have employed a simple equation to analyze ROI. This equation identifies the major determinants of investment return and can be useful in demonstrating why returns are increasing or decreasing. The formula is:

$$ROI = \frac{\text{Operating income}}{\text{Total assets}} = \frac{\text{Sales}}{\text{Total assets}} \times \frac{\text{Operating income}}{\text{Sales}}$$

Thus, return on investment is defined as the ratio of operating income to the assets tied up in the business; but this ratio is really composed of two other ratios: the asset turnover ratio (sales divided by total assets) and the operating margin ratio (operating income divided by sales). Essentially there are two ways to improve ROI. Either the entrepreneur can generate more sales per dollar of assets invested or he can increase the profit he earns per dollar of sales. A detailed analysis of the elements of this formula should play a major role in the firm's profit planning and control function. We summarize the determinants of sales, profit, and ROI growth in Figure 6-2.

Determinants of Growth and ROI for the Jackson Funeral Home

Ben Jackson has taken operating results for 1983 together with the balance sheet of December 31, 1983 (see Chapter 5) and calculated the ROI for that year. The result is:

$$ROI = \frac{\$14,727}{\$158,877} = \frac{\$154,032}{\$158,877} \times \frac{\$14,727}{\$154,032}$$

$$ROI = (0.97)(0.0956) = 0.0927 = 9.27\%$$

He sees immediately that his return on investment ensues from an asset turnover of 0.97 (i.e., he can generate $0.97 in revenues for

I. Determinants of Sales Growth
   A. Economic
      1. Overall economic activity
      2. Housing starts
      3. Consumer expenditures
      4. Business investment
      5. Interest rates
      6. Inflation
      7. Other
   B. Marketing
      1. Promotion
      2. Pricing
      3. Distribution
II. Determinants of Profit Growth
   A. Sales
   B. Cost of goods sold
   C. Selling expenses
   D. Administrative expenses
III. Determinants of ROI Growth
   A. Sales
   B. Profits
   C. Asset investment

Figure 6-2. Determinants of Growth.

each $1 of assets invested in the business) and an operating margin of 0.0956 (i.e., he can earn $0.0956 in operating income for every $1 in revenues generated). In order to improve his ROI, either his asset efficiency will have to be enhanced (generating more revenue per dollar of asset investment) or margins will have to increase (reducing expenses as a percentage of revenues). For 1984, improved asset efficiency is expected to raise ROI despite a decline in margins:

$$ROI = \frac{\$15,000}{\$151,700} = \frac{\$178,000}{\$151,700} \times \frac{\$15,000}{\$178,000}$$

$$ROI = (1.173)(0.0843) = 0.0989 = 9.89\%$$

Of course, Ben realizes that a major factor in improving his asset efficiency is the depreciation of his furniture, fixtures, equipment, leasehold improvements, and vehicles (see the planned balance sheet for 1984 in Chapter 5). Nevertheless, he is expecting to generate high revenue levels with this same equipment; hence, his asset turn-over improves.

In order to compute the ROI for 1985 to 1987, Ben will have to have both a planned operating budget (which he has prepared) and planned balance sheets. He knows that balance sheet projections are difficult to make but he does have some basis for evaluation. In the first place, his furniture, fixtures, and equipment are 5-year class assets and are being depreciated accordingly. Thus, depreciation for the $30,000 of FF&E purchased before he began operations would be:

Year	Rate of Depreciation	Dollar Depreciation	Value of Assets, End of Year
1983	0.15	$4,500	$25,500
1984	0.22	6,600	18,900
1985	0.21	6,300	12,600
1986	0.21	6,300	6,300
1987	0.21	6,300	0

Similarly, the $20,000 in leasehold improvements purchased before operations began would be depreciated as follows:

Year	Rate of Depreciation	Dollar Depreciation	Value of Assets, End of Year
1983	0.15	$3,000	$17,000
1984	0.22	4,400	12,600
1985	0.21	4,200	8,400
1986	0.21	4,200	4,200
1987	0.21	4,200	0

The $60,000 spent on vehicles (a 3-year class asset) would be written off according to the following schedule:

Year	Rate of Depreciation	Dollar Depreciation	Value of Assets, End of Year
1983	0.25	$15,000	$45,000
1984	0.38	22,800	22,200
1985	0.37	22,200	0
1986	0	0	0
1987	0	0	0

Thus, Ben could project his fixed asset investment to 1987, assuming no additional assets were purchased. This may be unrealistic, and it may be necessary to plan for the acquisition of new equipment. Let us suppose Ben feels it will be necessary to spend $10,000 on equipment, $10,000 on leasehold improvements, and $50,000 on new vehicles in 1987. The fixed assets section of his projected balance sheets for 1985 to 1987 would appear as follows:

	1985	1986	1987	
FF&E	$12,600	$ 6,300	$ 8,500	($10,000 less 15% depreciation)
Leasehold	8,400	4,200	8,500	($10,000 less 15% depreciation)
Vehicles	0	0	37,500	($50,000 less 25% depreciation)
	$21,000	$10,500	$54,500	

Next, Ben might attempt to calculate the amount of receivables and inventory he would have to carry during 1985 to 1987. This might be done by employing planned turnover levels. Thus, if he felt his collection period should average 60 days, his receivables should turn over $365/60 = 6.1$ times, and the level of receivables would be (assuming all sales are on credit):

Year	Revenues	Receivables Turnover	Level of Receivables
1985	$202,000	6.1	$33,100
1986	237,600	6.1	39,000
1987	291,800	6.1	47,800

Similarly, if merchandise were expected to remain on hand for an average of 90 days, the inventory turnover would be $365/90 = 4.1$ times, and the level of inventories would be:

Year	Cost of Merchandise	Inventory Turnover	Level of Inventories
1985	$36,400	4.1	$ 8,900
1986	42,800	4.1	10,400
1987	52,500	4.1	12,800

The remaining asset to be determined is cash, and this asset would essentially be a "plug" value depending upon what is done with the liability side of the balance sheet. In general, the retained earnings account should match the net income generated (less any dividend payments). The liability accounts would increase or decrease depending on financing assumptions, and the cash account would "balance" the balance sheets.

Given the above, Ben can compute his planned balance sheet for 1985 (see Table 6-3).

Notice that the asset accounts have been taken directly from the previous calculations. It was assumed that accounts payable would increase in accordance with the revenue increase anticipated from 1984 to 1985 (about 13.5%). Thus, budgeted payables of $4,373 from 1984 would rise to about $5,000. The note payable was assumed to remain at $20,000 while the scheduled reduction in the subordinated debt of $55,000 was taken into consideration. Planned net income of $3,600 reduces the retained earnings deficit from $12,673 in 1984 to $9,073. The remaining account required to "balance" the balance sheet would be cash. It would be expected to decline from the 1984 level of $60,000 to $37,927. Of course, if Ben felt this were an insufficient level, other financing might be arranged to raise the level of the cash balances.

It might also be worthwhile to reconcile the cash flow projected in the 1983–1987 Strategic Plan for 1985. The projected figure was negative: ($18,700). Nevertheless, the cash account went down by $60,000 − $37,927 = $22,073. The $3,373 difference may be traced to the $3,100 increase in receivables, the $900 increase in

Table 6-3
Jackson Funeral Home, Inc.
Planned Balance Sheet
December 31, 1985

Assets		Liabilities	
Cash	$ 37,927		
Receivables	33,100	Accounts payable	$ 5,000
Inventory	8,900	Note payable	20,000
FF&E	12,600	Subordinated debt	55,000
Leasehold	8,400	Common stock	30,000
Vehicles	0	Retained earnings	(9,073)
	$100,927		$100,927

inventories, and the addition of $627 in payables (a source of cash). Thus, $3,100 + $900 - $627 = $3,373.[6]

From his strategic plan, Ben can now determine planned ROI for 1985:

$$ROI = \frac{\$24,800}{\$100,927} = \frac{\$202,000}{\$100,927} \times \frac{\$24,800}{\$202,000}$$

$$ROI = (2.00)(0.1228) = 0.2456 = 24.56\%$$

For 1985, both improved asset efficiency and substantially higher margins result in a significant planned increase in ROI. Ben has repeated the procedure outlined above for 1986 (see Table 6-4).

Ben's 1986 ROI can be computed as:

$$ROI = \frac{\$58,400}{\$92,827} = \frac{\$237,600}{\$92,827} \times \frac{\$58,400}{\$237,600}$$

$$ROI = (2.56)(0.2458) = 0.6292 = 62.92\%$$

Table 6-4
Jackson Funeral Home, Inc.
Planned Balance Sheet
December 31, 1986

Assets		Liabilities	
Cash	$32,927		
Receivables	39,000	Accounts payable	$ 5,900
Inventory	10,400	Note payable	20,000
FF&E	6,300	Subordinated debt	0
Leasehold	4,200	Common stock	30,000
Vehicles	0	Retained earnings	36,927
	$92,827		$92,827

Cash Balance Reconciliation:	
Net funds flow	$ 1,500
Increase in receivables	(5,900)
Increase in inventory	(1,500)
Increase in accounts payable	900
Change in cash balance	($ 5,000)

[6] "Net cash flow" is often presented in operating statements as net income plus depreciation less debt payments. This will not necessarily equal the change in the cash account since this flow may be used to purchase assets (receivables, inventory, fixed assets). Also, any increase in a liability (payables, notes, etc.) would increase the cash balance. In this book, we use the term "net funds flow" for net income plus depreciation less debt payments and "net cash flow" for actual changes in cash balances.

Once again, for 1986, improved asset efficiency and much higher margins produce a substantial improvement in ROI.

In order to calculate ROI for 1987, it will be necessary to recompute the planned income statement to take into account the addition of assets that Ben felt he might have to buy in 1987. Clearly, a key factor in the ROI improvement from 1983 to 1986 is the ability of the firm to generate higher revenues with a depreciating asset base. At some point, additional assets will have to be acquired and the ROI should be expected to decline as these assets are "digested." Given Ben's assumption of buying $10,000 in equipment, $10,000 in leasehold improvements, and $50,000 in vehicles, the revised 1987 planned income statement would be as shown in Table 6-5. The planned balance sheet for 1987 would appear as shown in Table 6-6.

Table 6-5
Jackson Funeral Home, Inc.
Revised Planned Income Statement
December 31, 1987

Revenues	$291,800	[a]$214,000 + $15,500 in added depreciation.		
Cost of Services	229,500[a]	[b]Taxable Income	Rate	Tax
Operating income	62,300	$25,000	15%	$ 3,750
Interest expense	3,600	25,000	18	4,500
		8,700	30	2,610
Income before taxes	58,700			$10,860
Income taxes	3,200[b]	Credits		
Net income	55,500	Carry from 1986:		$2,703
Add: Depreciation	26,000	10% X $20,000:		2,000
Deduct: Debt pay-		6% X %50,000:		3,000
ment	20,000			$7,703
Net funds flow	$ 61,500	$10,860 – $7,703 = $3,157		

Return on investment for 1987 would be:

$$\text{ROI} = \frac{\$62,300}{\$129,627} = \frac{\$291,800}{\$129,627} \times \frac{\$62,300}{\$291,800}$$

$$\text{ROI} = (2.25)(0.2135) = 0.4804 = 48.04\%$$

Table 6-6
Jackson Funeral Home, Inc.
Planned Balance Sheet
December 31, 1987

Assets		Liabilities	
Cash	$ 14,527		
Receivables	47,800	Accounts payable	$ 7,200
Inventory	12,800	Note payable	0
FF&E	8,500	Subordinated debt	0
Leasehold	8,500	Common stock	30,000
Vehicles	37,500	Retained earnings	92,427
	$129,627		$129,627

Cash Balance Reconciliation	
Net funds flow	$61,500
Increase in receivables	(8,800)
Increase in inventory	(2,400)
Increase in FF&E	(10,000)
Increase in leasehold	(10,000)
Increase in vehicles	(50,000)
Increase in accounts payable	1,300
Change in cash balance	($18,400)

FINANCING LONG-TERM GROWTH

In Chapter 5, we discussed the major forms of short-term financing. We shall complete the discussion of financing a growth strategy here with a delineation of the major sources of long-term finance.

Term Debt

Term debt consists of loans with a maturity in excess of one year. Such loans are typically made by banks with maturities in the three- to five-year range, insurance companies with maturities in the five- to fifteen-year range, and other intermediaries (such as pension funds) for longer maturities. Term debt will often be secured with the fixed assets of the enterprise and will generally be made available upon the signing of a *loan agreement* that will have positive and negative covenants about the condition of the firm. A positive covenant is one that represents that the firm *will* do certain things — such as maintain a current ratio of 2:1 or better. A negative covenant is one that represents that the company *will not* do other things — such as pay a dividend while the loan is outstanding. Typical covenants include the following:

- Minimum working capital requirements
- Limits on capital expenditures
- Minimum liquidity requirements
- Limits on dividends, officer salaries, and stock repurchases
- Limits on the sale of assets
- Limits on the amount of additional debt that may be incurred
- Provisions preventing other creditors from obtaining senior status regarding asset or income claims
- Requirements for contracts with noncompete clauses for senior management
- Requirements for key man life insurance made out in favor of the lender

Term loans are usually repaid on an "amortized" basis. That is, a certain percentage of the loan is repaid periodically. Often, it is possible to borrow with a larger "balloon" payment due at the maturity of the loan. A typical 5-year term loan might thus call for 15% of the loan to be repaid in each of the first four years of the existence of the loan with a balloon for the remaining 40% at maturity.

Leasing

Although leasing is not commonly recognized by entrepreneurs as a source of financing, the accounting community now recognizes it as such. A lease is merely acquiring the use of an asset without having to purchase it. Thus, an automobile might be purchased by means of taking out a term loan for a three-year period. Alternatively, it might be leased over the same span. Instead of paying interest and having depreciation expense, the firm would make lease payments that would cover the cost of capital, depreciation, and a profit factor for the lessor. Many leasing companies make available "lease purchase" contracts whereby the leesee makes lease payments for a certain period of time and then can purchase the asset for its existing market value or some other specified sum. The accounting fraternity now requires that existing lease arrangements be capitalized under certain conditions. This arrangement "discounts" future lease payments at some appropriate interest rate (called a "capitalization rate"), and the resulting figure is added to the balance sheet as both an asset and an offsetting liability.

Bond Finance

Bond issues are similar in many respects to term notes but are more formal in nature. The essential difference between the two results from the fact that a term loan is usually negotiated with one lender whereas a bond issue is generally sold to an investment banker who, in turn, distributes it to the investing public. Because there are numerous lenders, it is necessary for them to have a representative. This representative is designated the "trustee" for the issue and is often the trust department of a bank or trust company. In place of the loan agreement, an "indenture" is drawn which specifies the rights and duties of the lenders and borrower. The indenture is negotiated by the borrower and the trustee as representative of the lenders. In the past, it was believed that the most secure type of bond was the mortgage bond. Mortgage bonds have a specific lien against property owned by the firm. It has come to be recognized, however, that interest and principal payments are made from income, not assets, and companies are increasingly able to sell unsecured bonds (debentures) on acceptable terms. Subordinated and junior subordinated debentures have even lower income and asset priority than senior debentures and are frequently sold as part of a package which may include equity "kickers" (see page 138).

Preferred Stock

Preferred stock is a curious combination of various features of debt and common stock. It is like common stock in that the instrument is called stock and is included in the equity section of the balance sheet. Also, payments to its holders are called dividends and are not deductible for corporate income tax purposes. The payment of preferred dividends is not legally required, and the issue normally has no fixed maturity. On the other hand, preferred stock is like debt in that the dividends usually have a fixed maximum rate. Preferred shareholders generally have no vote in the election of directors unless a specified number of dividends have been passed. Also, preferred stockholders are entitled to no more than the amount paid into the firm in case of liquidation. Although some entrepreneurs like to use preferred stock as opposed to "diluting" their equity position, it is an expensive form of finance. For a company in the 46% tax bracket, debt finance (term debt, leasing, bond issue, etc.) costs only 54% of the amount actually paid to creditors (the government picks up the 46% as a deduction). The full cost of the preferred dividend is borne by the company, however.

Equity "Kickers"

Frequently, when the entrepreneur borrows from a long-term lender, he will be asked to allow the lender to participate in the growth of the enterprise. This may be accomplished simply by letting the lender purchase some of the firm's common stock, or it may be done by making the debt "convertible." Convertible securities contain the option of being tendered to the company in exchange for its common stock. For example, an insurance company may have purchased $200,000 of ABC Corp. 12% bonds due in 1995. The bonds may be converted into 50,000 shares of ABC common stock at $4 per share. The *conversion ratio* indicates the number of shares that would be obtained from converting the bond (if the ABC bonds were $1,000 par value, each bond would be convertible into 250 shares). The *conversion price* is the par value of the bond divided by the conversion ratio (for the ABC bonds, this would be $1,000 ÷ 250 = $4).

Venture capitalists often like to lend to entrepreneurs and get *warrants* as their "kicker." A warrant is a legal instrument that allows its holder the right to purchase stock at a given price. Thus, a venture capitalist may be willing to lend the ABC Corp. $200,000 but would also require that warrants be attached to purchase 50,000 shares at $4 per share. This arrangement is not different from the previous one whereby the holder of the convertible security would give up his bond for 50,000 shares. In the case of the warrant, the venture capitalist would have to have his bond repaid (receiving $200,000) in order to exercise his warrant. Venture capitalists will often ask for warrants to buy stock at nominal prices. Thus, a venture capitalist might be willing to lend $200,000 but would want the right to buy 50,000 shares at $0.10 per share. This would allow him to get back his $200,000 investment as the bond (or note) is repaid and have an equity position for only 50,000 X $0.10 = $5,000. The entrepreneur should be careful about offering equity kickers, since he is effectively getting potential additional stockholders in the bargain.

Common Stock

The sale of common stock to raise money is the first source of finance obtained by the fledgling corporation. Typically, these funds will be supplied by the entrepreneur, although it may be necessary to allow others to participate if substantial sums need to be raised. Selling stock to others is like taking partners into any deal. It may be a good idea, and then again it may not. In the first place, if shares are sold to others, the equity of the entrepreneur is diluted. In the second place, minority shareholders can be a nuisance and can even instigate litigation if their rights are not scrupulously guarded. On the other hand, it may not be possible to raise money any other way. Also, some equity partners can be very useful. Venture capitalists, for example, may be far more than just investors and may supply the firm with much needed managerial and financial expertise. Furthermore, the presence of equity capital makes it easier to borrow and thus substantially more money may be raised if stock is made available to others.

Retained Earnings

As we suggested in Chapter 5, the principal source of finance to the firm that has gotten off the ground and is profitable may be the earnings it retains each year. This is the easiest source of finance to tap (assuming the company is making a profit) and requires no formalities (such as loan agreements, bond indentures, warrant agreements, etc.). All that is required to retain earnings is for the board of directors *not* to declare a dividend. It is that easy and that passive. Unless a dividend is declared (and there are few instances where a privately-held company should ever pay a dividend if it is growing and profitable), earnings are automatically retained.

Going Public

The decision to "go public" is beyond the scope of this book, but it should be noted that the entrepreneur who really wants his firm to grow may have no other choice. Nevertheless, going public is expensive and time consuming. A filing with the Securities and Exchange Commission may be required, and state "blue-sky" laws must be complied with. It may be necessary for the entrepreneur to give away a major part of his firm in order to sell shares to the public, and it is not uncommon for the accounting, legal, and underwriting costs of taking a firm public to absorb 20 to 30% of the proceeds of the offering. Alternatively, there are few better ways to allow a company to grow rapidly than by going public. In addition, many entrepreneurs have become very wealthy much quicker by having gone public. A public market for your stock improves the liquidity of your personal holdings, establishes a value for the major asset of most entrepreneurs (the stock in their company), and provides more acceptable collateral for borrowing. Furthermore, the entrepreneur may leave his heirs in far better condition by bequeathing them stock in a public company than a private one (which might have to be liquidated to pay estate and inheritance taxes), and the sale of some of his stock while alive may allow him to purchase other assets and thereby diversify his personal portfolio. Lastly, as we said earlier in this chapter, it may, in fact, be more enticing to own 15% of a public corporation worth $100 million than all of a private one worth $1 million! In any event, the decision to go public should not be made lightly. Once you have done it, it is hard to "go private" again. The best counsel and advice should be sought, and the entrepreneur should spend a lot of time analyzing the consequences of this decision.

Long-term Growth and Financing for the Jackson Funeral Home, Inc.

After having completed his revised strategic plan through 1987, Ben Jackson has summarized where he expects to be in four years. From beginning his firm from scratch a year ago, Ben anticipates having a business doing nearly $300,000 in volume by 1987. He intends to make almost $75,000 in pretax profits and be generating an ROI of about 50% on his asset investment. Moreover, during the five years that he will have been in business by 1987, he will have paid off *all* of the $130,000 he borrowed in 1982 and have a firm with a net worth of over $120,000. The outside investor who Ben solicited will have gotten his $110,000 in debt capital back and will still own 33.3% of the stock, while Ben will own 67.7%.

In the process of growing through 1987, the Jackson Funeral Home, Inc. will mainly employ internally generated funds. Accounts payable are expected to grow along with the increase in volume, but other sources of finance will be unnecessary. If Ben's plans work out, the business should have several options available to it in 1987. By having paid down all outstanding debt, the debt capacity of the company should be several hundred thousand dollars. Given the growth of the enterprise, outside stockholders could also be attracted to make possible expansion to additional locations. It is even conceivable that the firm could go public and begin an active acquisition program of other funeral homes. Ben could also exercise the purchase option he has on the mortuary property which continues to increase in value and carries favorable owner financing terms with a below market fixed interest rate for a 30-year mortgage. At the very worst, Ben believes his company will be worth at least $500,000 by 1987. This represents a multiple of less than seven times pretax income and just over four times book value – a conservative evaluation in Ben's mind. Thus, if Ben's plans are realized, the worst that could happen to him would be that he earned an attractive salary for five years, parlayed a $20,000 investment into $500,000, and had a great time in the process. The best that could happen – who knows? Ben has already thought about opening a new location or buying out one of his competitors in Wesson. He has even talked to his venture capitalist partner about putting up some more money. Fortunately, the plan for 1987 has just been put to bed. If 1984 turns out to be as good as expected, the strategic plan for 1985– 1988 might just require substantial altering from the 1984–1987 version.

SUMMARY AND CONCLUSIONS

In this final chapter we have demonstrated the exciting growth opportunities which may occur for an entrepreneur who establishes a business on a well-planned, sound basis and manages it efficiently.

The reader should reflect upon the Jackson Funeral Home experience as it unfolded: From the beginning, through its first year of operation, to the revised business plan extending to its fifth year of existence, Ben Jackson has been in control of his business rather than the reverse. He has established goals and objectives and adopted policies to achieve them. His detailed financial planning and intimate knowledge of all factors in his budgets are the key elements in his management control and resulting success.

Dr. Norman Hackerman, the president of Rice University, stated the following about his management style and philosophy in an address to the students of the Jesse H. Jones Graduate School of Administration: "One of the most important management techniques I have learned has been the importance of preparing your own budget and then measuring performance against it. If you prepare it yourself, or as it gets more complex, supervise its preparation directly so you know all there is to know about it, you are less likely to be surprised by irregular performance resulting from the actions of others."

If the entrepreneur starting a new enterprise (or the businessman managing an ongoing company) follows the principles and techniques discussed and illustrated in this book, his chances of being successful are certain to be enhanced substantially.

KEY TERMS

Asset Turnover Ratio. Sales divided by total assets. The asset turnover ratio is an indicator of the efficiency of a firm's asset investment.

Balloon Payment. A payment due at the end of a term loan that is normally larger than the periodic amount that would be required to pay off the loan over a given number of installments.

Blue-sky Laws. State laws regulating the issuance of securities within the individual states.

Bond Finance. Debt financing evidenced by the issuance of a formal contract (called an indenture) specifying the rights and duties of the lenders and the borrower. Bonds are generally sold to an investment banker who, in turn, sells them to the investing public.

Bond Indenture. A formal contract specifying the rights and duties of bondholders and the issuing company.

Bond Indenture Trustee. The representative of the bondholders who monitors the actions of the borrower to verify that the terms of the indenture are met. The bond indenture trustee is typically the trust department of a bank or trust company.

Capitalization Rate. An interest rate used to discount a future payments stream back to a present value.

Compound Growth. Growth calculations involving more than one period of time.

Conversion Price. The par or stated value of a convertible bond (or other senior security) divided by the conversion ratio (see below).

Conversion Ratio. The number of common shares that are obtained from converting a convertible security (see below).

Convertible Security. A bond or other senior security that has an option in its indenture allowing the security to be tendered to the issuing company in exchange for its common stock.

Economic Recovery Act of 1981. A tax act of historical dimensions that introduced major changes in U.S. fiscal policy.

Equity Kicker. Equity (common stock) participation added as a sweetener to a debt deal. Equity kickers may take the form of conversion privileges, warrants to buy stock, or other option rights.

Going Public. Selling a firm's stock to the general public.

ITCs. Investment tax credits. ITCs are allowed by the tax law to encourage business investment in plant, equipment, and other fixed assets. They represent a direct deduction from the firm's tax obligation.

Leasing. A means of acquiring the use of an asset without having to purchase it. Instead, periodic payments are made for the use of the asset.

Loan Agreement. A binding legal contract between a lender and borrower.

Loan Amortization. Periodic debt service (principal and interest) payments to repay a loan.

Negative Covenant. A term in a loan agreement that represents that the borrower will *not* do certain things (such as pay a dividend while the loan is outstanding).

Net Cash Flow. Net income plus depreciation flows less debt payments. Net cash flow will not necessarily equal the change in a firm's cash account over time since this flow may be used to purchase assets or repay liabilities.

NOLs. Net operating losses resulting from running a business. NOLs may be carried back 3 years or forward 15 years to offset previous or future income for tax purposes.

Positive Covenant. A term in a loan agreement that represents that the borrower will do certain things (such as maintain a specified current ratio).

Preferred Stock. A security combining various features of debt and common stock. Preferred stock is senior to the common stock but junior to all forms of debt in its claim on the income and assets of the issuer.

Retained Earnings. Earnings remaining (after the payment of dividends) which are reinvested in the business.

ROI. Return on investment. ROI is best determined for an operating business by dividing operating income by the value of the assets tied up in the business.

Term Debt. Loans with a maturity in excess of one year.

Warrant. A legal instrument that allows its holder the right to purchase a security (typically common stock) at a given price.

REFERENCES

Findlay, III, M. Chapman, and Williams, Edward E. *An Integrated Analysis for Managerial Finance.* Englewood Cliffs, NJ: Prentice-Hall, Inc., 1970.

Van Horne, J. C. *Financial Management and Policy,* Fourth Ed. Englewood Cliffs, NJ: Prentice-Hall, Inc., 1977.

Welsch, G. A. *Budgeting: Profit Planning and Control,* Fourth Ed. Englewood Cliffs, NJ: Prentice-Hall, Inc., 1976.

Weston, J. F., and Brigham, E. F. *Managerial Finance,* Seventh Ed. Hindsdale, IL: Dryden Press, 1981.

MATHEMATICAL APPENDIX TO CHAPTER 6

We may determine the compound growth rate formula as follows. Reconsider the simple growth rate equation:

$$X_1 = X_0(1 + G) \qquad \text{(Eq. 1)}$$

This may also be expressed as:

$$X_1 = X_0 + X_0 \cdot G \qquad \text{(Eq. 2)}$$

Furthermore:

$$X_2 = X_1 + X_1 \cdot G \qquad \text{(Eq. 3)}$$

We may substitute equation 2 into equation 3 to find:

$$X_2 = [X_0 + X_0 \cdot G] + [X_0 + X_0 \cdot G]G$$

which may be rewritten as:

$$
\begin{aligned}
X_2 &= X_0 + X_0 \cdot G + X_0 \cdot G + X_0 \cdot G^2 \\
&= X_0 + 2X_0 G + X_0 G^2 \\
&= X_0 (1 + 2G + G^2) \qquad \text{(Eq. 4)}
\end{aligned}
$$

The student of algebra will recognize at once that this can also be expressed as:

$$X_2 = X_0(1 + G)^2 \qquad \text{(Eq. 5)}$$

Similar substitutions could be made to show:

$$
\begin{aligned}
X_3 &= X_0(1 + G)^3 \\
X_4 &= X_0(1 + G)^4 \\
&\quad \cdot \\
&\quad \cdot \\
&\quad \cdot \\
X_n &= X_0(1 + G)^n \qquad \text{(Eq. 6)}
\end{aligned}
$$

Appendix A
TCI 1979 PARTNERSHIP
(Prepared September, 1979)

CONTENTS

Appendix A
TCI PARTNERSHIP

SECTION 1 INTRODUCTION

The TCI 1979 Partnership is composed of certain of the Directors and Advisory Directors of Trust Corporation International. The Partnership has the opportunity to purchase five railroad tank cars this year for investment purposes.

Railroad tank cars have historically been owned by users or private investors, such as the Partners, and there are a number of advantages to such ownership:

1. Railroad tank cars are a long-lived income producing asset.
2. Railroad tank cars afford an excellent hedge against inflation.
3. The tax benefits of tank car ownership afford an opportunity to control federal income tax expenses.

The railcars will be managed by Glenco Transportation Services, Inc., which assures they will be utilized as effectively as possible. The railroad tank cars being purchased are manufactured by a high-quality, experienced car builder, and they are general-purpose tank cars.

The estimated purchase price of the railroad tank cars is $242,500. The Partnership will finance the tank car purchases by providing $54,000 in contributed capital and by borrowing $196,000.

SECTION 2 A SUMMARY OF THE PROPOSED FINANCING

Borrowers: A newly-formed Texas partnership.

Credit facility: A term credit in the amount of $196,000.

Closing: A firm commitment from the lender is needed by October 31, 1979.

Terms: The notes will be repaid as follows: One payment of $5,348.71, on February 1, 1980; six quarterly installments of $8,580.72 beginning May 1, 1980; a balloon payment of $183,535.72 on November 1, 1981, which the lender has agreed to refinance over a ten-year period.

Security: The indebtedness will be secured by all of the railroad cars owned by the Partnership. Additionally, the management contract covering the tank cars will be assigned to the lender. The initial leases are for five years with Honeymead Products, a division of Farmers Union Grain Terminal Association, Inc. Farmers Union has an excellent credit history, maintaining a Dun & Bradstreet rating of 5A2. At the closing of its last fiscal year, Farmers Union had a net worth of $140 million with revenues for that year being $1.2 billion.

SECTION 3
TCI 1979 Partnership *Pro Forma* Combined Balance Sheet At Inception

Assets

Railroad tank cars	$242,500
Cash	7,500
	$250,000

Liabilities and partners' capital

Long-term notes payable	$196,000
Partners' capital	54,000
	$250,000

See accompanying notes.

TCI 1979 PARTNERSHIP
INCOME AND CASH FLOW ANALYSIS
PURCHASE OF FIVE TANK CARS

	1979	1980	1981	1982	1983	1984
Lease revenues	$	$ 30,300	$ 30,300	$ 30,300	$ 30,300	$ 30,300
Costs and expenses:						
Maintenance	—	5,455	5,455	5,455	5,455	5,455
Ad valorem taxes	—	910	910	910	910	910
Depreciation	22,250	37,125	30,940	25,780	21,485	17,905
Interest	3,827	24,344	26,566	25,400	24,058	22,515
	26,077	67,834	63,871	57,545	51,908	46,785
Taxable income (loss)	(26,077)	(37,534)	(33,571)	(27,245)	(21,608)	(16,485)
Add:						
Proceeds of loan	196,000	—	—	—	—	—
Income tax-savings contributed	50,327	7,155	10,391	10,391	10,391	10,391
Depreciation	22,250	37,125	30,940	25,780	21,485	17,905
Deduct:						
Purchase of tank cars	242,500	—	—	—	—	—
Principal payments	—	6,746	7,760	8,926	10,268	11,811
Cash flow	$ —	$ —	$ —	$ —	$ —	$ —

TCI 1979 PARTNERSHIP
NOTES TO *PRO FORMA* COMBINED FINANCIAL STATEMENTS

1. *Basis of presentation.*

    The accompanying *pro forma* financial statements represent the combined financial statements of the TCI 1979 Partnership which was formed to purchase five tank cars during 1979.

2. *Assumptions relating to the acquisitions.*

    a. The Partnership will acquire five railroad tank cars for approximately $48,500 each.

    b. The Partnership will finance the acquisition through the contribution of capital in the amount of $54,000 and by borrowing $196,000.

    c. The term borrowing of $196,000 will be repaid in seven quarterly installments and a balloon payment of $183,536, which the lender has agreed to refinance over a ten-year period. The first such installment of principal will be due on February 1, 1980. The borrowing will be secured by the railroad tank cars owned by the Partnership together with the management contract.

3. *Assumptions relating to the pro forma combined statement of operations and cash flow.*

    a. The Partnership accounts for leases under the operating method. The total purchase price of the railcars leased is recorded as an asset; rental revenues, depreciation on leased property, management fees and other related costs are reflected in the accompanying pro forma combined statement of operations.

    b. The Partnership has leased the five 20,800-gallon cars initially for a term of five years at $505 per month per car.

    c. The initial indebtedness of the Partnership will bear interest at a rate of 14.25% for its two-year term. The refinanced balance will bear interest at the rate of prime plus .75%.

    d. For financial statement purposes, depreciation will be computed on the basis of the estimated useful lives of the tank cars, 40 years, by the straight-line method. For income tax purposes and in the accompanying statement of operations, depreciation is provided using a twelve-year life and the double-declining balance method.

    e. The maintenance fee will be 18% of lease rentals; ad valorem taxes will approximate 3% of lease rentals.

    f. The Partners will contribute out of their respective tax savings each year, a sum sufficient to amortize the debt. Such amount equals approximately $10,400 per year, except for 1980, when a smaller amount will be contributed. Funds to meet the first installment of debt due February 1, 1980, were included in the initial contribution of capital.

SECTION 4 THE PROPOSED TRANSACTION

History of Tank Car Operations

The private ownership of tank cars is a well-accepted concept in the railroad industry. Unlike other types of rolling stock, tank cars are not normally owned by the railroads.

At the present time, there are approximately 170,000 railroad tank cars in use in the United States. A very small percentage of such tank cars is owned by the railroads and they are used primarily for the movement of their own supplies and materials. The other tank cars are owned or controlled by private interests outside of the railroad industry.

Historically, the American railroads have not furnished special-purpose vehicles to shippers or other users of railroad equipment. Thus, the nation's railroads have not acquired and do not furnish tank cars for the movement of bulk liquid commodities by rail. In 1888, the Interstate Commerce Commission (ICC) agreed with the railroads that it was economically unsound for each railroad to maintain enough tank cars to satisfy the needs of its shippers and at that time, the private car lines were born.

Since the shipper-owned cars were producing revenues for the railroads, it was further ordered by the ICC that the shippers be reimbursed for the cost of the cars; this was accomplished by the payment of mileage allowances to the car owner. This practice has been continued with the current mileage allowances being divided basically into six (6) different rate categories. The categories are determined principally by the age and original cost of the car.

When a shipper forwards a loaded tank car furnished by him, the shipper pays the railroad a published tariff charge to cover the cost of movement, including the cost of providing the car. The railroad then pays the car owner an amount equal to the loaded miles traveled multiplied by the applicable mileage rate. If the car is leased by the shipper from a Tank Car Leasing Company, the mileage is paid by the Railroad to the Lessor (Car Owner) who in turn passes the mileage credit to the Shipper (Lessee) to be used by the shipper as a reduction in his cost for furnishing the car.

Advantages of Railcar Ownership

The private ownership of railcars affords an excellent hedge against inflation. Increases in the price of new tank cars and their resulting lease rates have at least been equal to, and in most instances, exceeded the rise in the consumer price index during the recent past.

The following table compares the percentage increase in the rentals of a general purpose tank car with the corresponding increase in the consumer price index:

	Tank car rental, per month	Percentage increase in tank car rental	Percentage increase in CPI
1975	$329	—%	—%
1976	415	26	6
1977	425	3	7
1978	450	6	8
1979	525	17	13[a]
		52%	34%
Average for the period		13%	9%

[a]Projected.

Due to the combination of low obsolescence and inflation, many types of railcars have actually experienced an appreciation of their market value during the past fifteen years. The Interchange Rules of the Association of American Railroads provide the method for determining the settlement value the owner is to receive in the event the car is destroyed in an accident. Such specification shows, for example, that a tank car purchased new in 1973 would today have a settlement value equal to 134% of its original cost; a 10-year old tank car would have a settlement value of 145% of original cost. While these settlement values do not necessarily equal actual used values for a tank car, they do indicate that a railcar is an appreciating asset.

The Wholesale Price Index for Iron and Steel and the price of a new tank car compare as follows:

COMPARISON OF THE INCREASE IN THE COST OF A 20,800-
GALLON INTERIOR COILED, NONINSULATED TANK CAR TO THE
WHOLESALE PRICE INDEX CODE 101, IRON AND STEEL

	Average car cost		
	Amount	Percent increase over base year	Code 101 Average[a]
1969 (Base year)	$19,000	100.0%	100.0%
1970	22,000	115.8	115.1
1971	23,400	123.2	121.8
1972	24,800	130.5	118.4
1973	25,500	134.2	136.2
1974	34,400	181.1	178.6
1975	36,000	189.5	200.9
1976	38,600	203.2	215.9
1977	42,000	221.1	230.4
1978	45,000	236.8	253.5
1979	48,500	255.3	272.0[b]

[a] Bureau of Labor Statistics Wholesale Price Index for Iron and Steel.
[b] Index for January 1, 1979.

Ownership of railcars by the Partnership allows the partners to effectively manage their federal income tax expense. The cars generate investment tax credit equal to 10% of their original cost, and additionally, may be depreciated on an accelerated basis for tax purposes.

The Manufacturer

All of the cars are being purchased from the General American Tank Car Company (GATX), of Chicago, Illinois. GATX, with nearly a century's experience, is a quality manufacturer of rail cars. The cars will bear the serial numbers GLNX 21106, 21107, 21108, 21109, and 21110.

The Equipment

The equipment being purchased consists of the following:

Quantity	Description
5	20,800 gallon, general-purpose, nonpressure tank cars, DOT 111A100W1, interior coiled and noninsulated.

Tank car specifications are developed by the Association of American Railroads (AAR), and the Department of Transportation (DOT). Part 179, Title 49,

Code of Federal Regulations provides for four general categories for tank car specifications as follows:

1. Subpart C — Specifications for Pressure Tank Car Tanks
2. Subpart D — Specifications for Nonpressure Tank Car Tanks
3. Subpart E — Specifications for Multiunit Tank Car Tanks
4. Subpart F — Specifications for Liquefied Hydrogen Tank Car Tanks

The tank cars being purchased fall into the first two categories — pressure and nonpressure tank cars. The tank cars built to specification DOT 111A100W1 are authorized for shipment of a wide range of low-pressure products and are classified as "general-purpose" by the industry.

Proposed Operation of the Cars

The cars will be managed for the Partnership by Glenco Transportation Services, Inc. (Glenco) pursuant to a Management Agreement, a form of which is included herein (omitted).

The services to be provided by Glenco include the following:

1. Using its best efforts to obtain the most favorable terms and rentals for the cars throughout the term of the Management Agreement.
2. Collecting rental and service charges earned by the cars.
3. Filing all registration and other reports required by governmental or industry agencies or commissions, including filing ad valorem and other tax returns.
4. Maintaining books and records pertaining to the cars.
5. Providing at Glenco's expense, all repair and maintenance work required by the cars.
6. Providing quarterly reports of the operations of the cars to each owner.
7. Maintaining general liability and property insurance in designated amounts.
8. Collecting and remitting mileage credits to Lessees.

The management fee payable to Glenco under the Management Agreement is 18% of the lease rentals and service charges earned by the cars.

All ad valorem, property, or similar taxes levied against the cars and all other tank cars owned or managed by Glenco will be aggregated and allocated among such tank cars based on the rental income and service charges earned by the tank cars.

Glenco continually contacts shippers to solicit lease business. Glenco maintains a file of shippers derived from various industry and governmental publications. In addition, Glenco, from time to time, expects to receive inquiries from a number of shippers. The principal leases are expected to be with shippers of bulk commodities such as oils, fuels, chemicals, and food products.

Leases covering some of the cars presently owned or managed by Glenco are with the following high quality lessees:

Mobay Chemical Company
Lubrizol Corporation
Exxon
Sun Oil Company
Union Carbide Corporation
SCM/Durkee Foods Company
Allied Chemical Company
Phillips Petroleum Company
Shell Oil Company

All moves by tank cars, whether loaded or unloaded, are reported to Glenco by each Lessee and are also followed by AAR computer movement reports, including the various railroads on which the tank cars move. When a car leaves the factory, an identification number is placed on the car for registration with the AAR. A record is maintained containing all information obtained from the railroads and from the AAR, which converts loaded mileage movements into cash receivables. The receivable amount is compared to the revenue received from the railroad. In addition to the complete mileage movement history, an income history is kept on each car. Repairs and maintenance histories are also kept on each car. With such histories, Glenco can determine if any car is developing a recurring problem which might indicate that a repair is needed. Glenco also maintains records of Lessee activity, routing destination and commodities carried. Glenco uses the mileage movement history to prepare and file ad valorem, property, gross receipts and other tax returns.

Glenco prepares invoices on a regular monthly basis for all tank car leases and acts as the owner's agent in collecting all income, including mileage allowances. Glenco maintains records sufficient to account properly for all income and expenses applicable to the operation of the cars. Glenco provides the owners with quarterly reports detailing lease income and expenses allowed under the Management Agreement (including Glenco's fee and any capital improvements required by regulation).

Tank Car Leases to Shippers

Glenco will make arrangements with shippers for use of the cars. Glenco will enter into tank car service contracts (commonly referred to as leases) in accordance with and subject to the Interchange Rules promulgated by the AAR and substantially in the form of a lease included elsewhere herein. The tank car service contracts provide for payment of rentals and indemnification by the user in the event of damage caused by or to the tank car or damage to its contents.

In the tank car industry, lease agreements with shippers are for various terms. Glenco will attempt to obtain medium-to-long term leases for the cars. It will use its best efforts to enter into arrangements with shippers for use of the cars for terms of not less than 36 months. Medium-term leases usually command a lease rate which is higher than long-term leases and also provide a greater inflation hedge.

There are several methods by which an owner can be compensated for the use of tank cars. The principal basis for compensation is a fixed minimum rental rate, established in advance in the lease contract with a shipper and determined by the length of time the tank car will be used and the nature of the commodities to be carried.

Another method of compensation is through retention of the mileage earned by the cars. As previously described, the railroads pay a mileage credit to the car owner.

Based on prevailing market conditions, the management of Glenco believes it is in the best interest of the owners to lease the nonpressure cars on terms which will range from two years to six years, and to lease the pressure cars on initial five- to six-year terms.

New Car Guarantee and Inspections

New tank cars must be built to the AAR Tank Car Specifications, DOT Tank Car Specifications, and the AAR Specifications for the design, fabrication and construction of freight cars. The specifications must be approved by the AAR Tank Car Committee before the cars can be built and placed in service. The AAR and DOT specifications are the result of extensive research and testing and reflect standards established by the American Society for Testing and Materials, the American Society of Mechanical Engineers, and other recognized national organizations. The cars have a warranty against defects in materials and workmanship from the General American Tank Car Company, the car builder, for one year. Extensive inspection and testing is performed by GATX prior to delivery.

Repairs and Maintenance

Repairs to new tank cars have typically been of a minor nature, generally confined to running gear equipment such as brake shoes, brake repairs, couplers, etc. The repairs usually range between $10 and $200 per occurrence and their frequency is related to usage of the car. Major repairs exceeding this amount are very infrequent during the first seven years of service.

In the eighth year, the Federal Railroad Administration ("FRA-DOT") requires that the car be taken out of service for certain inspections including the basic running gear of the car — brakes, couplers, center plates, wheels, etc. All of the required repairs will be made to the car, including painting and tank and safety valve testing when appropriate. The cost of the repairs is covered by the management fee and is paid by Glenco. Any design changes or other modifications required by governmental regulations are paid by the car owner but the cost of such improvements is recovered through an increase in rentals, as provided in the lease agreement.

It should be noted that improvements to the cars through technological changes are normally made over the life of the car by making repairs with improved parts. In this manner, the cars are kept in good running and operating condition without incurring abnormal costs. Prior to loading, a car must be inspected to insure that the tank and fittings are in proper condition for the safe transportation of the lading. After loading, the car must be inspected by the carrier to see that it is not leaking and that the air and hand brakes, roller bearings, trucks, etc., are in proper condition. There are also federal requirements for inspections during movement to assure the car is in good operating condition. In 1970, the DOT passed regulations limiting size and weight of tank cars. Part 179.13 states "Tank cars built after November 30, 1970, must not exceed 34,500 gallons capacity or 263,000 pounds gross weight on rail. Existing tank cars may not be converted to exceed 34,500 gallons capacity or 263,000 pounds gross weight on rail." Therefore, for light weight products, the gallonage capacity has been limited to 34,500 gallons capacity and for heavier products the weight has limited the size to a total of 263,000 pounds on the rail. It has also been determined by the AAR that in order to increase the load limit on the railroads over the 263,000-pound limit, it will be necessary to spend billions of dollars to upgrade the track, roadbeds, etc. The capacity of the cars being purchased both from a gallonage and weight standpoint, are the maximum which is allowed for transportation of products normally shipped at present and for the foreseeable future. All of these cars meet and exceed the latest DOT specification requirements.

The low-pressure cars are equipped with sloping bottom tanks to allow for more rapid and complete unloading; exterior heater coils to provide for heating and better unloading of viscous products and an inner tank which can easily be interior lined and cleaned; four (4) inches of fiberglass insulation which provides protection against rapid change in temperature and allows for a minimum of heat loss and amount of time necessary for reheating for unloading; top and bottom unloading arrangements which allows for the unloading of the cars through the top or bottom fittings in a closed system thereby allowing shippers to comply with the federal and state EPA loading and unloading requirements; top and bottom shelf couplers which aid in preventing the couplers from becoming disengaged and puncturing other tanks in case of rail accidents. These cars are ideal for the petroleum, fertilizer, food, and chemical industries.

The pressure cars are equipped with the latest safety design requirements of the DOT:

1. Top and bottom shelf couplers as discussed above.
2. 1/2-inch thick steel insulation jacket heads to assist in preventing tank head punctures in case of accidents.
3. 1/2-inch thick 6-lb density ceramic fiber insulation next to the outer tank shell to provide for thermal insulation in case of an accident and fire.
4. 1 3/4-inch urethane foam insulation as required by the 105 specification which also provides for greater product stability and protection.

Insurance

Glenco will maintain property insurance on the cars with limits of coverage of not less than $57,000 per car, $250,000 each occurrence, with no more than a

$5,000 deductible each occurrence, naming each owner and secured lender as additional insured.   Loss resulting from damage or destruction of the cars will generally be covered by the railroad on which the cars are operating, or by the lessee.

SECTION 5 THE TCI 1979 PARTNERSHIP

The TCI 1979 Partnership consists of certain of the Directors and Advisory Directors of Trust Corporation International. The Partnership has been formed to engage in a mutually beneficial transaction which will serve to cement the business relationship shared by the Partners in their respective roles within Trust Corporation International. A brief sketch of the background and experience of the Partners of the TCI 1979 Partnership is provided below:

(Names and background of the partners omitted.)

Appendix B
AMPAK DRILLING INCORPORATED
AND
AMPAK LEASING COMPANY
A Limited Partnership
(Prepared February, 1981)

CONTENTS

Appendix B
AMPAK DRILLING INCORPORATED
AND
AMPAK LEASING COMPANY
A Limited Partnership

SECTION 1 INTRODUCTION

Ampak Drilling Incorporated (ADI) will operate as a drilling contractor using equipment leased from Ampak Leasing Company (ALC), a limited partnership formed to provide assets for use by ADI, and to give private investors the benefits of investing in the oil industry by purchasing limited partnership interests in ALC. Ten are available at $50,000 each.

Presently there are several key advantages to investing in oil field equipment for individual investors through a limited partnership.

1. They are high income producing assets and provide excellent security for debt.
2. The tax benefits of ownership due to accelerated depreciation and investment tax credits afford an opportunity to control federal income tax expenses.

The estimated purchase price of this oil field equipment is $1,873,330. The Partnership will finance the purchases by providing $500,000 in contributed capital and by borrowing $1,400,000. The equipment will then be leased to ADI for a reasonable rental which will cover the necessary servicing of debt of ALC.

This is one of several limited partnerships that Ampak wishes to form. Within 2 years the company will control eight rigs and have revenues in excess of $10 million.

SECTION 2 THE INDUSTRY

The drilling contractor industry is presently characterized by specific entry opportunities into shallow well drilling operations of 4000–8000 feet. New entrants are capable of high growth due to the highly fragmented industry and the demand for services which far exceeds the number of rigs available. Growth rates in the industry since 1973 have been spectacular for contractors in these categories and the wide range of services and equipment required offer good diversification possibilities into related areas. With the prospects for continued deregulation, to encourage exploration and production of domestic oil and gas supplies, and a continued energy shortage for the next decade, the drilling contracting industry has a better outlook than ever seen in the past.

THE COMPANY

Ampak Drilling Incorporated will be formed to operate drilling rigs and related oil field equipment leased from Ampak Leasing Company, a limited partnership. It will be an independent contractor performing drilling and workover operations for operators in the Texas, Oklahoma, Kansas and Louisiana areas in shallow well operations from 4000–8000 feet. Company emphasis will be on offering premium service with premium equipment exercising efficient drilling technique. By doing this a stable niche will be earned in a growing market which will protect Ampak as much as possible from market volatility allowing high growth rates in the drilling industry and the potential for diversification.

PROPOSED FINANCING FOR AMPAK LEASING COMPANY

Sources of Funds: $500,000 contributed capital by limited partners through the sale of ten $50,000 limited partner interests. $1,400,000 term credit.

Terms: The notes will be repaid over ten years with 15% interest on the outstanding principal. Amortization will be based on a constant loan payment.

Security: The debt will be secured by all of the assets owned by Ampak Leasing Company which amount to $1,873,330 subject to an amount of $100,000 to be borrowed on a 10% partnership interest held by Ampak Drilling Incorporated.

PROPOSED FINANCING FOR AMPAK DRILLING INC.

Borrower: Ampak Drilling Incorporated.

Credit Facility: A term credit for the amount of $100,000.

Closing: A firm commitment is needed from the lender by March 1, 1981.

Terms: The note will be repaid over ten years in equal installments of $10,000 with 15% interest on the outstanding principal.

Security: The note will be secured by a 10% general partnership interest in Ampak Leasing Company which contains assets of $2,000,000.

SECTION 3

Ampak Leasing Company 1981 Partnership
Pro Forma Combined Balance Sheet
At Inception

Assets

Ideco drilling rig	$ 427,138
Ideco mud pump unit	314,114
Related equipment	
See Section 7 (omitted) for listing	1,132,078
Cash	26,670
	$1,900,000

Liabilities and Partners' Capital

Long term notes payable	$1,400,000
Partners' capital	500,000
	$1,900,000

See accompanying notes.

Ampak Drilling Incorporated
Pro Forma Balance Sheet
At Inception

Assets

Cash	$110,000

Liabilities and Equity

Long term notes payable (secured on partnership interest)	$100,000
Common stock ($1.00 par)	10,000
Total liabilities and equity	$110,000

See accompanying notes.

Ampak Drilling Incorporated
Pro Forma Income Statement

	June–Dec. 1981	1982	1983	1984	1985
Percent utilization	90	85	80	80	80
Revenues	$756,000	$1,224,000	$1,152,000	$1,152,000	$1,152,000
Cost of sales					
Fuel	151,200	244,800	230,400	230,400	230,400
Wages	235,872	381,888	381,888	381,888	381,888
Maintenance	60,000	60,000	60,000	60,000	60,000
Equip. rental	192,500	330,000	330,000	330,000	330,000
Total Cost	639,572	966,688	952,288	952,288	952,288
Plus mgmt. income	29,167	50,000	50,000	50,000	50,000
Gross margin	$145,595	$257,312	$199,712	$199,712	$199,712
Salaries	60,000	100,000	100,000	50,000[a]	50,000
Income from operations	$85,595	$157,312	$99,712	$149,712	$149,712
Income (loss) from leasing company	(27,319)	(41,172)	(26,585)	(12,990)	(4,274)
NIBT	$58,276	$116,140	$73,127	$136,722	$145,438
Taxes	(11,732)	(34,174)	(16,188)	(43,642)	(47,652)
Investment tax credit	11,732	7,001			
Net Income	$58,276	$88,967	$56,939	$93,080	$97,787

[a]By this year administrative expense should be spread over multiple rigs.

Ampak Leasing Company
Pro Forma Income Statement

	1981	1982	1983	1984	1985	1986	1987	1988
Rental revenues	$192,500	$330,000	$330,000	$330,000	$330,000	$330,000	$330,000	$330,000
Mgmt. expense	29,167	50,000	50,000	50,000	50,000	50,000	50,000	50,000
Depreciation	312,222	487,846	353,394	230,584	158,526	82,919[a]	82,919	64,920
Operating income	(148,889)	(207,846)	(73,394)	49,416	121,474	197,081	197,081	215,080
Interest expense	(122,500)	(203,875)	(192,456)	(179,324)	(164,223)	(146,857)	(132,188)	(116,830)
Net income (loss)	($271,389)	($411,721)	($265,850)	($129,908)	($42,749)	$50,224	$64,892	$98,250
After Tax Cash Flow Assuming 50% Tax Bracket Limited Partner								
Cash inflow	$ 40,833	$ 76,125	$ 87,543	$100,675	$115,777	$133,143	$147,812	$163,170
Amortization of debt	40,833	75,125	87,543	100,675	115,777	97,989	102,388	94,395
Cash from operations	0	0	0	0	0	35,154	45,424	68,775
Tax	0	0	0	0	0	(25,112)	(32,446)	(49,125)
Tax benefits of loss	135,694	205,860	132,925	64,954	21,374	0		
Investment tax credit	187,333							
Total benefit	$323,027	$205,860	$132,925	$ 64,954	$ 21,374	$ 10,042	$ 12,978	$ 19,650
For a 70% bracket taxpayer[b]	$377,305	$288,204	$186,095	$ 90,935	$ 29,924	0	0	0

This gives a 18.32% rate of return over 8 years for a 50% bracket taxpayer or a 33.86% rate over 5 years for a 70% bracket taxpayer.

[a]Change to straight-line depreciation.
[b]In 1986 change to straight-line method.

Notes to Pro Forma Combined Financial Statements

1. *Basis of Presentation*

   The accompanying *pro forma* financial statements represent the combined statements of Ampak Leasing Company, a limited partnership formed to purchase oil field equipment and Ampak Drilling Incorporated, the general partner of ALC which leases the equipment for its operations. ADI has a 10% interest in ALC.

2. *Assumptions Relating to the Acquisitions*

   a. Ampak Leasing Company will acquire oil field equipment at a cost of $1,873,330.

   b. The Limited Partnership, ALC, will finance the acquisition through $500,000 of contributed capital and debt of $1,400,000 (borrowed at 15% and repaid over ten years).

   c. The equipment is leased to Ampak Drilling Incorporated for a set sum of $280,000 per year.

3. *Assumptions Relating to the Pro Forma Combined Statements of Operations and Cash Flow*

   a. The partnership accounts for leases under the operating method. The total purchase price of the equipment is recorded as an asset with related rental revenues and depreciation on the leased property.

   b. ALC will depreciate the property over seven years using double declining balance methods switching to straight line depreciation in year four, assuming a salvage value of $100,000.

SECTION 4 AN OVERVIEW OF THE DRILLING INDUSTRY

The oil industry is composed of the following principal segments:[1]

- Exploration
- Drilling
- Production
- Transportation
- Refinery/petrochemical operations

The segment of interest is drilling, in particular, contract drilling. Oil companies usually employ contract drilling companies to do their exploration and development drilling rather than own and operate the equipment and manage crews themselves. In a recent survey by *Drilling* magazine,[2] operators and contractors were asked why oil companies preferred contract drilling. In most cases the reasoning was identical. The principal reasons that emerged are given below:

---

[1] Wheeler, Robert R., and Maurice Whited: *Oil — From Prospect to Pipeline,* Third Ed., Gulf Publishing Company, 1975.
[2] Mayborn, Ted W. "Why Oil Companies Use Contract Drilling," *Drilling,* No. 525, September, 1980.

- Capital tied up in drilling equipment
- Writing off contract drilling expense
- Obsolescence factor in owning drilling equipment
- Multiplying company accounting, buying equipment, and paying crews
- Hiring and training drilling crews
- Maintaining personnel records
- Need for a variety of rig sizes
- Need for using rigs in widely separated areas
- Recognition of contractors' expertise in his area or region of operation.

Basically the need for contract drilling firms as opposed to oil company ownership emerged during the mid-1930s and grew rapidly during and after World War II. Flexibility was a major advantage for expanding oil companies who wanted to be at several different areas at once, with a variety of rig sizes. When the oil companies began to shed their rigs many a drilling superintendent became an early day contractor.

A drilling contractor is considered to be a "specialist" in his field and operators prefer to let professional drillers do the drilling. T. B. Garber, Cola Petroleum, Inc., wants to continue in the role of oil/gas producer: "We are developers and producers. With capital requirements for rig ownership, the advantage of writing off contract expense, the problem of hiring crews — plus the need for being able to drill in different areas, we prefer to contract for our drilling."[3]

The 1980s have been termed the "golden decade of drilling." There has been a 30% increase in completions during the first six months of 1980 over the same period last year. The American Petroleum Institute says 11,578 oil wells were completed during January–June 1980 as compared to 8,582 in 1979. The 3,000 mark for rotary rigs running in the United States has been broken three times by Hughes Tool Company's weekly count. The first time was in 1950 when a high count of 3,021 was pegged. It happened in 1955 when an all-time record of 3,137 rigs were counted turning to the right. And it happened on August 18, 1980, when a Hughes rig count of 3,050 was recorded. Hughes recently reassessed its estimate of the weekly average of rigs running in 1980, placing the new figure at 2,850, well ahead of the record 2,600-plus level of the mid-1950s (see Table 1).

Table 1 How U.S. drilling activity will increase

	1979	1980	1981
Active rigs*	2,177	2,850	3,200
Wells	51,263	59,475	66,500
Footage (million ft)	243.2	284	321.6
Average well depth (ft)	4,744	4,775	4,836
Footage/rig	111,717	99,650	100,500

*Average for the year

3 "Contract Drilling is Here to Stay," *Drilling*, No. 525, September, 1980.

Most forecasts and market studies estimate final totals after year-end showing an all-time high of just over 60,000 wells drilled in the U.S. in 1980, surpassing the record of 58,478 wells drilled in 1956. Smith International, Inc., expects 64,000 holes to be drilled in 1980 with a forecast of 68,500 holes and more than 300 million feet of hole for 1981.[4] A projected 75% rise by 1990 in U.S. oil and gas drilling is predicted by the Bankers Trust Company of New York in a recently published forecast for 1980–1990.

Texas operators reported 83 gas and 40 oil discoveries during the first two weeks of August 1980 compared with 53 gas and 28 oil discoveries in that period the year earlier. $51.95 per foot is the average cost of drilling an oil well in Texas, according to Texas Mid-Continent Oil and Gas Association. That is a 238% increase from 1970.

Dr. Anthony Copp, Vice President of Solomon Brothers, New York based investment bankers, told the recent joint IADC-PESA[5] marketing seminar audience that his company's overall view of the industry is for a near tripling in size in terms of sales and assets by the end of the 1980s.[6]

The table below is based on a sample of 22 drilling companies and their consolidated performance between 1971 and 1978.

Table 2

	Percent Change 1978 over 1971
Sales	+256
Assets	+290
Operating income	+387
Net income	+378
Operating margin	-7.6

The downward trend in operating margin reflects increased competition.

Ed McGhee, executive vice president of the International Association of Drilling Contractors, reported earlier this year (1980) that rig utilization exceeded 90%.

The drilling contractor's market is divided into two types of operators: the first type of customer is the large integrated oil company or the large independent. These operators have the staff, resources, and capability to manage their own drilling operation and take rigs on "day work." The second type of customer is characterized as the small independent, who lacks a staff equipped to make decisions on drilling operations. He wants the contractor to do it all, from making bit selections, to getting the location ready, to handling third-party services.

---

[4] "No Letup in Sight for Big Surge of Drilling in U.S.," *Oil and Gas Journal*, October 20, 1980, p. 93.
[5] International Association of Drilling Contractors–Petroleum Equipment Suppliers Association.
[6] "Massive Borrowing Seen for Drillers," *Drilling Contractor*, December 1979, pp. 24–25.

The operator generally considers that the contractor with the newer, better maintained equipment will do a better job. Other selling factors include superior training of the personnel. For this purpose the Association of Oil Well Servicing Contractors, and Howell Training Corporation have produced training films and aids. These along with on-the-job experience complete the basic training of the crewmen. An advanced school for toolpushers and crew chiefs is held six times a year in Odessa and will soon also be held in Houston and Kilgore, Texas. This school is organized by Petex (Petroleum Extension of the University of Texas). In addition, the AOSC sponsors safety clinics and seminars on a regular basis.

Drilling has become a good independent investment and rig availability is tight. Contractors own and operate 99% of all domestic drilling rigs. The prospects are bright overseas too as rig count in the free world approaches 5,000. Drilling contractors in 1979 received nearly $8 billion of the oil companies' total expenditures in drilling and completing wells.

SECTION 5 AMPAK DRILLING INCORPORATED

Ampak Drilling Inc. will be in a highly fragmented industry where there are many one-rig contractors. The main distinction among these contractors is their equipment and this is what sells the contractors' services. Marketing is taken care of due to the nature of the industry. Oil operators desiring to drill oil wells must file intent to drill notices with state corporations commissions. These are published by industry publications or are available from the state. The contractors then contact the operators in the notices and offer their services. Once agreed upon, a contract as exhibited in Section 6 is composed (omitted). These contracts often cover multiple well sites in a general area, and presently the demand is such that new rigs are commanding multiyear contracts. The equipment used by ADI is of such a premium nature and capability that heavy demand will be experienced. Industry surveys have shown that greatest demand will be for rigs of ADI's type. The time of Ampak's two officers will be spent alternating between drilling sites and marketing the services of ADI.

The emphasis of ADI will be on marketing, cost control, and expansion. Presently many contractors are of low educational levels and are inherently myopic in their view of the market. The officers of ADI have a distinct advantage in this respect due to their financial and technical backgrounds. Cost control will be affected by use of advanced drilling monitor equipment which will help assure efficient drilling rates with minimum loss of drilling fluids and low formation damage. This equipment is included in the itemized list of Section 7 (omitted). Also, it is felt that an officer should be on the site at all times to supervise crews and in case of stoppages. Due to remote locations and 24-hour-a-day drilling schedules the two founders will alternate on two-week schedules. When not on the drill site they will do marketing and other duties for ADI. This devotion of time will ensure the success of Ampak Drilling Incorporated.

(The remainder of the plan consists of the resumes of the principals).

Appendix C
Electric Cars of Houston
Summary Financing Plan (Loan Proposal)
August, 1981
Prepared By:
BRAINTRUST INCORPORATED
Houston, Texas

TABLE OF CONTENTS

Appendix C
Electric Cars of Houston
Summary Financing Plan (Loan Proposal)

OVERVIEW

Electric Cars of Houston (ECH) is a proposed business venture that evolved over the past year among a group of individuals who realized a need in the marketplace for an automotive related business which meets the needs of the customer from a quality, reliability, and fair-price point of view. The profit centers for the business have been designed to include proven markets such as conventional internal combustion used-cars, long-term leasing, automotive repair service, and tires and auto parts. Another dimension of the business would be the retail and service of new electric vehicles which is slowly making an entry into the transportation market and which research reveals will make a substantial penetration into the automotive market in the near future. ECH considers its entry into this field of transportation as a timely, strategic, and profitable business decision based on the present state-of-the-art of electric vehicle design, economy, future energy situation, and the changing needs of society.

The owner/manager team of ECH is cognizant of the initial inherent risk of supporting a part of the business on electric vehicle sales and service. As a result, the owners have agreed to totally absorb the risks of the business by offering their personal financial statements and assuming personal liability to the full amount of the loan of $200,000. Thus, the lending institution will have the personal assets of the owners as collateral against the loan amount. Additionally, in spite of the conservative sales forecasts, the business is projected to be highly profitable (*pro forma* income statements and cash forecast for 3 years are attached) and the total loan will be repaid by the fourth year of business.

The success of any business is largely dependent on the management and entrepreneurship ability of the people in the business. ECH has a team of successful and experienced professionals with a substantial background and knowledge of the automobile industry and professional management in order to make this business successful. The conviction of the business will be "to satisfy customer needs at a profit to the business."

This loan proposal outlines the purpose and objectives of the loan, proposed method of financing, profile of owners/management, basis of sales forecasts, profit potential and loan repayment schedule, personal financial statements, resumes, and *pro forma* statements of the business. Also included is a brief note on electric vehicles that gives information on the product, present and future market, and the research and development that is being done to make EV's viable alternate mode of personal and business transportation.

PURPOSE AND OBJECTIVES

Electric Cars of Houston (ECH) is a proposed new business venture backed by a group of financially strong, highly talented, successful, and experienced individuals who are motivated by the good profit potential of an automotive dealership which will have the following characteristics:

1. To be located in an affluent and high growth metropolitan area of the country.
2. To provide high quality, fast, courteous, and fair-priced automotive services.
3. To meet the needs of the average auto service customer who is generally dissatisfied with the quality of presently available services.
4. To make an entry into a high-growth and promising field of future transportation which will overcome the problems of availability and price of gasoline and provide a better quality of life in terms of pollution and noise.

Within the guidelines as just mentioned, ECH has been designed to operate as a professionally managed, diversified (controlled risk), and full-service automobile dealership to be located in Houston's boomtown environment. New electric vehicles will be sold and serviced, specialized high-quality and profitable auto repair service will be offered for conventional internal combustion vehicles, fast, while-you-wait lubrications will be featured, replacement parts will be retailed, used vehicles (mostly conventional) will be traded for and merchandised, auto leasing and daily rentals will be offered, financing and insurance will be arranged, tires will be marketed, and auto detailing/clean-ups will be performed.

The proposed dealership will be established with minimum capital investment to maximize the flexibility and cash-flow that would be very important during the early stages of its operation. The working capital loan of $200,000 would supplement $35,000 of equity to provide a total starting capital of $235,000.

The material provided in the subsequent sections of this proposal describe the desired method of financing as well as substantiate the loan on both a collateral basis as well as an ability to service and repay the debt within the first four years of operation.

PROPOSED METHOD OF FINANCING

The proposed capital structure of the business is as follows:

(a) Owner's equity (7 investors @ $5,000 each) $ 35,000
(b) Debt (Loan secured by personal financial
   statement of each of the 7 investors) $200,000
      Total Capital $235,000

The loan of $200,000 is proposed to be secured by the following:

(a) The personal net worth of each of the seven investors. An amount of $28,571.43 will be personally guaranteed by each investor against their individual personal assets covering the total amount of $200,000.
(b) In addition, the initial inventory of $60,000 is to be acquired with the loan, comprising both used gasoline power vehicles and automotive parts/tires, which will also be offered as collateral. This inventory will consist of the following:

Item	$ At cost
Used cars	$25,000
Auto parts: electric	$10,000
gasoline	$10,000
Tires	$15,000
Total beginning inventory	$60,000

OWNERSHIP AND MANAGEMENT

Electric Cars of Houston's owners firmly believe in, and will practice professional management in conducting all aspects of its business. The owners and Board of Directors are comprised of individuals with a diversity of talents — several with extensive automotive backgrounds. Each member of the group has been highly successful in their professions, are aggressive and committed to make a success of this business venture. The Board will also serve as an active management group, and will be involved in all major planning and decision making. A summary of the individuals involved follows:

Name	% Ownership	Position	Profession/ Background
1. (Names omitted)	One-seventh (14.3%)	President and Chairman of the Board	Ten years of entrepreneurial and auto-retail experience.
2.	One-seventh (14.3%)	Vice President and Director	Management Consultant/Broad range general business; extensive factory and dealership automobile experience.
3.	One-seventh (14.3%)	Treasurer and Director	CPA/partner in accounting practice.
4.	One-seventh (14.3%)	Secretary and Director	Owner of Construction firm.
5.	One-seventh (14.3%)	Director	Four years of entrepreneurial and auto-retail experience. Business graduate.
		Director	Management Consultant. Five years of engineering and business experience.
6.	One-seventh (14.3%)	Director	Entrepreneur/Investor
7.	One-seventh (14.3%)	Director	

BUSINESS DIVERSIFICATION AND RISK MANAGEMENT

A major consideration in the business design of Electric Cars of Houston has been the minimization of risk. This has been done in two ways. First, the income of the business has been diversified over five different profit centers and second, the sales forecasts have been kept extremely conservative. The bases of sales forecasts have been explained in the next section of this proposal and a summary of the income diversification of the business is shown below:

Profit Center #	Profit center	Gross Profit					
		1st Year		2nd Year		3rd Year	
		$	Total	$	Total	$	Total
1.	New electric vehicles	344,400	43%	720,000	42%	756,000	39%
2.	Service — all vehicles	180,000	23%	432,000	25%	504,000	26%
3.	Used vehicles — gasoline	121,500	15%	237,600	14%	288,000	15%
4.	Parts — all vehicles	106,800	13$	259,200	14%	302,400	15%
5.	Tires	46,800	6%	86,400	5%	100,000	5%
Total Gross Profit		$799,500	100%	$1,735,200	100%	$1,950,400	100%

	Net Profit After Taxes		
	1st Year	2nd Year	3rd Year
Total Net Profit After Tax	$ 52,319	$ 385,651	$ 472,310

What happens to the business if the actual sales of electric vehicles are far below the forecasts? This is a logical question, as it relates to a new venture with a product line that is new to the market and for which the actual sales potential has not yet been proven. The management of Electric Cars of Houston has thoroughly considered this possibility, and have concentrated upon a multiplicity of income building profit centers with products/services which have proven markets. With such diversification the business should be profitable in any eventuality. The Electric Vehicle Sales Department contributes approximately 40% of total income. Thus, in a hypothetical case, assuming that no electric vehicles are sold, the business will still be profitable each year, and will still achieve 60% of the projected net profits after tax. However, as was mentioned before, there are various reasons to believe that Electric Cars of Houston will not only meet the projected sales forecasts, but should excel in all profit centers.

The management of Electric Cars of Houston is cognizant of both the sales potential of electric vehicles in Houston, and also the profit potential of a well managed and professionally designed automotive dealership such as planned for ECH. *The total risk of the business is being absorbed by the investors* in the form of a guarantee for the loan amount against their personal financial statements. The lender is, therefore, totally safe from any risks of the business.

BASIS OF SALES FORECAST

The credibility of *pro forma* income statements and cash forecasts of any business is largely dependent on the accuracy of sales forecasts of the business. The sales forecasts for ECH has been done after extensive research and are conservatively estimated. Similarly, the expenses for the business have been compiled after a detailed analysis of every conceivable expense for starting and running an automobile dealership.

The following is a description of the background data and primary research that was done to arrive at the sales forecasts:

1. ELECTRIC VEHICLES:

Electric Vehicles Sales Projection for Houston, Texas

Current Monthly Auto Sales for Houston (Vehicles)[a]	Projections for Electric Vehicle Market Share[b]	Projected Vehicle Sales per Month		
		1st Year	2nd Year	3rd Year
		(Assuming No Market Growth)		
14,700	Low 0.1%	15	15	15
	High 2%	294	294	294

Electric Cars of Houston Monthly Sales Projection

	1st Year	2nd Year	3rd Year
	14	30	35

Sources: [a]"Selected Indicators" Houston Magazine, June 1981, p. 6. Houston Chamber of Commerce.
[b]"EV Commercialization — What Is Making It Happen". Anthony H. Ewing (DOE), Electric Vehicle News, Nov., 1980, p. 6.

It may be noted that the current and future potential for electric vehicles as a percentage of the total vehicle population is presented as a range based upon average figures employed within the industry. Houston is expected to achieve a higher percentage. Reasons for this include the high concentration of industry and commerce which will serve as a major component of EV sales, and the large segment of the population in the upper income, education, age, and family size ranges which fall within the demographic buyer profile for consumer EV sales. The warm weather and flat terrain of Houston are also most desirable environmental conditions for operation of EV's.

2. USED VEHICLES: The used vehicle market in Houston is presently very strong according to a survey of local retailers. Because of the high cost of new vehicles and the cost of borrowing, many "would be" new car buyers are purchasing used vehicles for more affordable payments. The demand for exceptional used vehicles consistently exceeds the supply. In addition to trading for the used vehicle industry, ECH will purchase vehicles from other dealers and from vehicle owners in Houston and other areas. Also, vehicles will be handled on consignment for owners. These sources will assure an adequate supply of vehicles. Used vehicle sales are expected to be limited only by the level of inventory which can be afforded.

3. SERVICE: Primary data was collected from auto dealerships and independent and franchised service centers. The demand for auto service is directly related to the increasing number of vehicles entering the market — which is experiencing dramatic growth.   Consumer inquiries indicate that many vehicle owners are dissatisfied with the impersonal and inconsistent quality of auto services being offered by the large metro dealerships and service centers.

Projections for service income for ECH have been taken very conservatively, and are based on a limited number of service technicians — only two initially. The location at 4303 San Felipe is designed to accommodate approximately 15 technicians — who will be added as volume dictates. In addition, this location in the River Oaks area is expected to provide excellent prospects for drive-in service based upon the high volume of traffic (traffic count 31,421 as of 8/6/80), and the assumption that area residents can afford and desire to properly maintain and service their automobiles.

4. PARTS SALES: Parts sales are directly related to the volume of service being performed. Standard industry guidelines have been employed to estimate this component of income. Parts sales will be comprised of both electric vehicle parts (which will not be available from other sources) and from parts sold in the repair of conventional vehicles.

5. TIRE SALES: Tire sales will provide another profit center and will further diversify the income of the business and will establish ECH as a full-service operation. Because of the additional battery weight in the EV's, tire wear will occur faster than with conventional vehicles. This, therefore, justifies the need for competence and a product offering of tires for internal reasons. Also, the convenience of a tire company will benefit neighborhood residents and other

passers by.   Income from tire sales has been taken very conservatively, after conducting research with tire distributors and dealers.

PROFIT POTENTIAL AND LOAN REPAYMENT SCHEDULE

The projected profitability of the business and cash balances at the end of each year of the business is summarized below:

	1st Year	2nd Year	3rd Year
Net profit after tax for the year before dividends.	$ 52,319	$385,651	$472,310
Cash balance on last day of the year after loan payments, but before dividends.	$137,319	$312,970	$605,280

Due to the strong profitability and accumulated cash balances of the business, ECH proposes that the loan repayment be scheduled as follows:

Repayment in the 2nd year	$ 50,000
Repayment in the 3rd year	100,000
Repayment in the 4th year	50,000
Total	$200,000

The debt service for each year has been included as an expense in computing the net profit and cash balances for each year.

(Please refer to the Financial Data Section of the Business Plan)

ATTACHMENT 1
GENERAL INFORMATION ON ELECTRIC VEHICLES

"Seldom in the process of any human endeavor is it possible to know, at the time, when a success threshhold has been crossed.   Historical perspective is always more accurate if the historian has the *courage of objectivity*.   So it is, I am certain, with the entrance of the electric vehicle into the personal and fleet automotive markets.   That point of convergence of the factors required for production of electric vehicles as a consumer product may have already been crossed.   Among the driving forces which determine the potential profit for the product, the balance of the importance has clearly shifted from technology to economics: now it is no longer "will it run," but "how much will it cost."   Price not performance is the hurdle to be crossed." (*Electric Vehicles News,* May 1981, p. 10)

The above quotation seems to be an accurate assessment of the state-of-the-art of electric vehicles and its potential as a realistic transportation alternative. Probably unknown to the general public and to the majority of the gasoline-vehicle users, the government has been contributing approximately $37 million per year over the past few years, and private industries have expended many more times that amount into research and development of electric vehicles as a viable alternative to the gasoline-fueled vehicle. (Rich Ceppos, "Driving by Wire," *Car & Driver,* June 1981, p. 44.) This is an outcome of the world's present energy situation and the new attitudes which are evolving. This outline is a summary of some of the significant aspects of electric vehicles – characteristics, benefits, and limitations.

1. WHY ELECTRIC VEHICLES?

The world energy situation has been recently plagued by uncertainties relating to both availability and cost of petroleum as a major source of energy. The United States imports about 40% of its crude oil of which roughly half is consumed by automobiles. Our government is therefore committed to developing alternate sources of energy for powering automobiles, and at the same time, reduce dependence upon foreign countries.

Because of the increasing demand for economical vehicles major companies like General Motors have made huge investments in researching alternative fuels for future vehicles. (Rich Ceppos, "Driving by Wire," *Car & Driver,* June 1981, p. 44.) The demand for, and potential proftis in this market have been a major motivator to companies in developing electric vehicles.

Why electricity? Most energy observers feel that synthetic fuels are at least fifteen to twenty years away and, at present, electricity is by far the most attractive energy source in terms of cost and availability. The future supply of electricity is projected to be stable in price and availability due to the majority of electricity producing plants being fueled by coal. Very conservative estimates place America's coal reserves to last at least a couple of thousand years even at triple the rate of present consumption (National Coal Association's estimates). Technological advances in emission equipment has made it possible to burn coal cleanly, and coal's potential as a raw energy source is virtually limitless.

With the present electricity generating equipment in the country, 60 million electric vehicles could now be charged during off-peak hours at night. This capacity is more than adequate considering the number of EVs forecast through the 1980s.

From an energy conservation point of view, the electric motor drive is also more attractive than gasoline-fueled engines. In general, the electric motor runs at 75% efficiency, while gasoline engines operate at 20% efficiency.

The other advantages are reduction of air pollution in urban areas and lower traffic noise.

2. MARKET FOR ELECTRIC VEHICLES

Presently the market for electric vehicles is dominated by industrial and commercial users. It is estimated that vans and trucks occupy a major share of the total vehicles produced to date.

In 1980, approximately 2,000 electric vehicles were sold, and figures are expected to go up to 100,000 by 1990 and 900,000 by 1995 as forecast by Predicasts Inc., a Cleveland, Ohio based market research firm (*Automotive News,* Sept. 8, 1980).

The potential market for electric vehicles for consumer application is expected to be comprised of two- and three-car families who will employ the electric vehicle for short-range commuter driving. Presently there are an estimated 35 million gasoline cars which are used for short-range driving and could be replaced by EVs. (*Automotive News,* Sept. 8, 1980.)

The present individual consumer demand for electric vehicles comes primarily from affluent or curious individuals. The future demand is expected to increase as a result of rising gasoline prices and reduced availability; and, greater practicality of EVs based upon research to reduce initial and maintenance cost, improved range, reliability, and charging characteristics.

The limited range of electric vehicles is countered by the facts discovered by the Department of Energy in a 1979 study which showed that a car with daily range of 82 miles could meet travel needs on 95% of days. Ordinarily after a day's drive, the owner would plug the electric vehicle into a handy outlet so that the car will be fully charged within 6 to 10 hours.

3. COST

Most electric vehicles' purchase cost is approximately 50% more than the comparable gasoline-fueled models, but the cost per mile of the electric vehicle is only 30 to 50% that of the gasoline vehicle.

At higher volumes of production the initial cost of electric vehicles will be cost competitive with conventional vehicles and still provide its other advantages.

The lower operating cost for electric vehicles is due to the low cost of electric energy and also due to lower maintenance costs — no engine tune-ups, muffler, catalytic converter, oil and engine coolant changes, etc. The motor will operate practically trouble-free for over 20 years with only an annual check of the motor brushes.

4. PRODUCT

An electric vehicle accelerates smoothly and provides essentially the same handling characteristics as conventional autos while being substantially quieter. Most vehicles have a cruising speed of 55 miles per hour (mph) and a maximum speed of 60 to 70 mph.

Air conditioning and automatic transmission are available in some models.

Most electric vehicles have a range of up to 60 miles at cruising speeds of 35 to 45 mph with the present commercially available battery technology. With recent developments in advanced battery technology, vehicles have been tested that give a range of up to 150 miles. (More on batteries in next section.)

After approximately 30,000 miles, the present batteries need replacement at a cost of approximately $1,200. One of the new types of batteries that are being tested will last the lifetime of the vehicle without any replacement.

5. BATTERIES

Presently an adapted version of the familiar lead-acid battery is being used for all electric vehicles. Research in batteries is being done to develop a new system designed to store vastly more energy within the same weight and volume occupied by present batteries. Also, batteries are under development which will not require replacement during the life of the vehicle.

General Motors is testing a nickel-zinc battery that will occupy half the volume and will weigh half as much as the lead-acid battery for the same amount of energy. This would double the range of the present vehicles. The only drawback of this battery is the limited life of about 300 cycles of recharging at 120 miles per charge giving a total life of 36,000 miles.

Gulf & Western is testing a zinc-chlorine storage system (battery-equivalent) which can provide 150 miles of range at a speed of 55 mph on a single 8-hour charge for a compact automobile. This system will also have a high recharging life of 1,400 cycles which gives a total battery life of 210,000 miles — more than the lifetime of a normal car. This battery would not need replacement.

At the laboratory stage of development are aluminum-air batteries which are self-consuming, power-generating energy cells. This system uses aluminum, air, and water to generate its own electricity and should go about 1000 miles before it needs to be refueled with fresh aluminum electrodes. (Rich Ceppos, "Driving by Wire," *Car & Driver;* June 8, 1981, p. 46–47.)

6. LIMITATIONS OF ELECTRIC VEHICLES

The limitations of electric vehicles are centered around the battery technology due to the higher volume, higher weight, limited range between charges, limited life of batteries, unfavorable power characteristics below freezing temperatures, and the time required for recharging. Some of these are direct causes for the higher cost of the vehicle and are indirectly due to the limited present demand not permitting manufacturers to gain the cost advantages of economies-of-scale. The recent developments in battery technology are encouraging and future research and engineering are expected to overcome these limitations.

Electric Cars of Houston
Business Plan

Contents

Electric Cars of Houston
Business Plan

I. Background

Electric Vehicles have been in use since 1837, when Robert Davidson of Aberdeen, Scotland, built the first one. By 1912, a peak of 33,842 electric vehicles were in use when Charles F. Kettering developed the electric starter for Cadillac gasoline-engined cars. This overcame the hand cranking drawback and catapulted gas powered vehicles ahead of electrics. (*Car & Driver,* "A Quick Jolt of History," June, 1981, p. 51–52.)

Electrics are now making another comeback as a result of high costs and uncertain availability of gasoline. Both private industry and government are spending substantial sums on EVs to make them viable as alternate modes of transportation. Although the industry is expected to prosper from the mid-1980s, a notable demand for EVs is evident today in consumer and industry segments.

Products are presently available which offer speeds of up to 70 mph, 70+ mile ranges, air conditioning, and automatic transmission. The limited range is expected to be overcome in the near future by new batteries which are presently being tested by GM and Gulf & Western.

Although an element of risk is involved in the commercialization of EVs, it is believed that we are presently in the embryonic stages of an industry which will be vitally involved in future transportation. The benefits are expected to greatly offset the risks.

II. The Business

A. *Description*

Electric Cars of Houston (ECH) has been designed to operate as a diversified full service automobile dealership. New electric vehicles will be sold and serviced, specialized high-quality auto repair service will be offered for conventional internal combustion vehicles, replacement parts will be retailed, used vehicles will be traded for and merchandised, auto leasing and daily rentals will be offered, financing and insurance will be arranged, tires will be marketed, and auto detailing/clean-ups and ten-minute oil changes will be performed.

Because of the number of profit centers involved, the store will be self-sustaining even in the unlikely eventuality that electric vehicles are not received as expected. The strength of all departments will flow from the management's understanding of the automobile business and more specifically knowing how to fulfill customer needs and preferences and to provide complete satisfaction, at a profit to the company. Therefore, success of ECH will result from providing a true alternative to the typical "run-around" ordeal of purchasing an auto and having it properly serviced and maintained. The customer orientation, organization of all aspects of the operation, quality line of products and services offered, and caliber of personnel attracted will distinguish ECH as a leader in commercial and consumer transportation in the Houston marketplace.

B. *Market*

At present, the potential for electric vehicle sales is projected at between 0.1 and 2% of the total auto market, by most analysts ("EV Commercialization — What Is Making It Happen," Anthony H. Ewing (DOE), *Electric Vehicle News*, Nov., 1980, p. 6). Market share estimates rise appreciably and have been projected to 7.35% by 1995 by one source (Research Group, Predicasts, Inc. *Automotive News*, September 8, 1980). Other sources project 25% market share by the year 2000 ("Driving by Wire," *Car & Driver*, June, 1981, p. 44).

Currently, for 1981, an average of 14,699 vehicles per month are being retailed in Houston (first quarter 1981, *Houston*, June, 1981, p. 6). Estimating EV sales within the 0.1 to 2% range would provide potential sales of between 15 and 294 vehicles per month for the Houston market. Sales for ECH have been projected at a fraction of this potential market since monthly sales of 4 to 25 per month have been conservatively forecasted with only 164 new units for the first year of operation.

The potential for success for EVs in Houston is expected to far exceed projections. Reasons for this include the high concentration of industry and commerce which will serve as a major component of EV sales, and the large segment of the population in upper income, education, age, and family size ranges which fall within the demographic buyer profile for consumer EV sales.

Houston is one market in the country where EVs are easily suitable since the flat terrain and moderate year around temperatures are most desirable. The only major drawback for Houstonians — limited range upon a charge is expected to soon be overcome with the new battery technology under development which should provide ranges of 200 to 300 miles before a recharge. Present technology has a zinc-chloride battery system with a range of over 150 miles (*Car & Driver*, "Driving by Wire," June, 1981, p. 46). These new batteries will also be adaptable as replacements to those currently in use. Present vehicle range of up to 70 miles per charge is considered adequate for the average application since research shows that an average of 80 miles are driven daily by 90% of the U.S.

population of vehicle operators (*Car & Driver*, "Driving by Wire," June, 1981, p. 46).

As a result, Houston is expected to be a leader in the acceptance and use of electric vehicles as an alternate mode of transportation.

C. *Competition*

ECH will compete in general with all new and used vehicle dealerships, with independent and franchised service and tire outlets, and rental and leasing agencies. Because of the size of the potential market and in consideration of the company's business philosophy and unique product and service offering, a reasonable niche in the total market may be expected.

Direct competition on electric vehicles is expected in the future but not initially. At present ECH has dealer selling agreements with Jet Industries, the major supplier of EVs in the country, and with The Electric Car Company.

These manufacturers provide a diversity of products designed to meet consumer preferences. Having two strong suppliers will also lessen business risk and better ensure product availability, will reduce potential competition, and will establish ECH as a leader and authority as an exclusive EV dealership.

General Motors is the only major auto manufacturer which presently appears to be preparing to enter the EV market in a major way in 1985–1986. It is not presently known whether their products will be sold through existing dealers or whether a separate dealer network will be established. However ECH will have an estimated four- to five-year advantage and experience to enable it to counter strong competition. Also ECH's management will closely follow the product acceptance curve for EVs and will remain abreast of the present and expected markets for its products. At an optimum point in the market, ECH's management would consider selling the operation for a substantial gain. This would, of course, be weighed against the benefits of a long-range income earning potential, tax considerations, and the investor's objectives.

D. *Location*

ECH has negotiated a lease for a facility located at 4303 San Felipe just two blocks east of the 610 Loop. The surrounding River Oaks neighborhood is expected to create a favorable and strong image for the dealership. In addition, this area of high-income residential and business concentration is expected to provide substantial clientele for the operation.

The dealership is a modern brick facility with large offices, a six-car showroom, approximately 15 service bays, and ample lot space for vehicle display and customer parking.

E. *Personnel*

The attached Organization Chart (omitted) and resumes (omitted) describe the positions and individuals who are now committed to key roles. Since the dealership's target date for operation is December 1, 1981 — it is not yet practical to make firm commitments to attract employees. Because ECH's management has substantial auto background, a number of personal contacts are under consideration for various roles in the operation.

The Board of Directors and Advisors is comprised of individuals with a diversity of talents — several with extensive automotive backgrounds. This group is highly committed to the success of electric vehicles, and of Electric Cars of Houston. The Board will serve as an active management group and will be involved in all major planning and decision making. In some cases, Directors will also share in the ownership of the firm.

The firm's management has conducted extensive research into the EV industry and products, and have been aggressively involved in this project since Sept., 1980. Four EV manufacturers, throughout the U.S., have been visited, and technical schools were attended.

F. *Products/Services*

a. *Electric Vehicles*

The EV product line presently consists of subcompact autos, small pickups, conventional half-ton pickups and half-ton window and cargo vans as offered by Jet Industries under the Electra nameplate. These vehicles are derived from the Ford Escort/Mercury Lynx, Ford Courier, and Dodge Ram pick-ups and vans. These vehicles are purchased and converted by Jet.

The Lectra product line from The Electric Car Company consists of conversions of Datsun cars and pick-ups and are well-engineered products.

The importance of having more than one supplier is for purposes of lessening risk, maximizing sales through greater product availability, reducing competition, and gaining recognition as an exclusive EV operation — rather than selling EVs alongside conventional vehicles.

b. *Used Vehicles*

Used vehicles offered by the dealership for retail sale will be only clean, recent models with low mileage. This will enhance customer satisfaction and will enable extended warranties and financing to be offered. Older model or poor condition trades will be wholesaled.

c. *Tires*

Cooper tires are presently being considered because of their high quality construction and reasonable price. Also, direct competition is limited for this brand.

Tire sales provide an excellent profit center and enable the sale of additional parts and services including: shocks, suspension parts, brakes, wheel balancing, tire rotation, front-end alignment, etc.

d. *Leasing/Rentals*

New EVs will be leased over a 2-, 3-, or 4-year period. The leasing department will be set up and operated in the same manner as conventional leasing operations. This will enable a broader segment of the market to be satisfied and will provide ECH with additional sales.

Also, EVs will be rented on a daily basis. This will provide another profit center for the store and will act as a sales tool for prospective buyers who want to try the products before buying.

e. *Service*

Comprehensive service will be provided for EVs for both warranty and non-warranty repairs. Also light, high-profit service will be performed on conventional vehicles.

f. *Parts*

Parts will be sold for internal repairs and at retail for consumers desiring to maintain their vehicles.

g. *Finance/Insurance/Warranty*

ECH will offer internally arranged bank financing and insurance as a customer service. This will also facilitate the sale of more vehicles and will provide an additional income source.

An extended warranty will be offered on both new and used vehicles which will provide another profit center.

G. *Marketing*

In addition to proper display, well-trained and courteous sales representatives, a good inventory of products, and the proper image for the store, various types of promotion are being developed.

Aside from a professional internal sales staff, an outside sales rep will call on industrial and commercial fleet operators. Marketing data such as that published by Dun & Bradstreet, which describes local fleet operators, and the types of vehicles in operation will be employed to further identify potential customers for direct mail and personal contact.

Also, public awareness activities will include free publicity in all local media. This encompasses public and private television – public interest, news, and talk programs; local newspapers and periodicals; and radio. Public and private exhibits and displays will be conducted at shopping centers, airports, hotels, trade shows, parades, rodeos, and sporting events (Astrodome), etc.

A fleet of demonstration vehicles will be employed for test drives by individuals and businesses, and will be made available to churches, high schools, universities, trade schools, and for driver's education purposes. Presentations to groups and meetings will be made regarding the concept and practicality of the EV. Conventional fee-paid advertising will be employed in various media to supplement publicity.

H. *DOE Program*

The U.S. Department of Energy is sponsoring a program subsidizing the cost of an electric vehicle to the purchaser or lessee. The purpose of this program is to promote the EV as an alternative to the conventional vehicle and to enhance its market acceptance. Benefits from this program would be substantial to the program operator/dealer. ECH has applied to the DOE for participation in the program and is presently under consideration. However, the present status of the program is in question as a result of the DOE's budget cuts under the new administration.

I.   *Investor Group*

Working capital of $235,000 is required for Electric Cars of Houston to become operational (see Cash Forecast).   Such an amount is required for the projected level of operations in order to maintain adequate cash balances.

The investor group will consist of seven investors who will invest $5,000 cash apiece and will offer their signatures to secure a financial statement loan of $200,000, and a line of credit for new vehicle floor planning of $250,000. The floor plan will be secured by the new vehicle inventory which is to be insured.

Six of the seven investors are already committed, and the seventh is under consideration.   A number of prospective investors have expressed their willingness to participate as the seventh investor.   ECH would make the final selection based on the financial strength, professional background, and compatibility of the seventh with the existing investor group.

Each investor will have equal (one-seventh) ownership of ECH in terms of common stocks issued by the company.   The Chairman of the Board and President of the company will, however, control 51% of the voting stock to facilitate efficient management and control of the operational matters of the company.

(Organizational chart, resumes, and financial statements of investors omitted.)

Electric Cars of Houston
Pro Forma Income Statement Sept., 1981 Thru Aug. 1984 (3 years)

Profit Center	Sales	1981 Sept.	Oct.	Nov.	1981 Dec.	1982 Jan.	Feb.	March
1.	New — Electric vehicles — $	56,000	70,000	98,000	126,000	154,000	168,000	196,000
	— Units	4	5	7	9	11	12	14
2.	Used — All Vehicles — $	20,000	25,000	30,000	40,000	50,000	60,000	60,000
	—Units	4	5	6	8	10	12	12
3.	Service — Labor $	10,000	14,000	18,000	19,000	20,000	21,000	24,000
4.	Tires	5,000	5,000	7,000	7,000	9,000	9,000	10,000
5.	Parts-Service/retail/wholesale	6,000	9,000	11,000	12,000	13,000	14,000	15,000
	Total $	97,000	123,000	164,000	204,000	246,000	272,000	305,000
	Gross Profit							
1.	New — Electric vehicles	8,400	10,500	14,700	18,900	23,100	25,200	29,400
2.	Used — All vehicles	3,600	4,500	5,400	7,200	9,000	10,800	10,800
3.	Service — Labor	6,000	8,400	10,800	11,400	12,000	12,600	14,400
4.	Tires	2,000	2,000	2,800	2,800	3,600	3,600	4,000
5.	Parts/service/retail/wholesale	3,600	5,400	6,600	7,200	7,800	8,400	9,000
	Total	23,600	30,800	40,300	47,500	55,500	60,600	67,600

Expenses

		1981 Sept.	Oct.	Nov.	1981 Dec.	1982 Jan.	Feb.	March
A.	Salaries/commissions — staff New Electric Vehicle — comm.	2,100	2,600	3,600	4,700	5,700	6,300	7,300
	Used vehicle — comm.	900	1,100	1,400	1,800	2,200	2,700	2,700
	Mechanics — (40% commission +)	1,000	1,400	300	2,400	2,000	1,600	2,900
	Porters	1,600	1,600	1,600	1,600	1,600	1,600	1,600
	Salespersons parts/tires	1,500	1,500	1,500	1,500	1,500	1,500	2,300
	Salaries — Supervision General manager Sales manager	3,500	3,500	3,500	3,500	3,500	3,500	5,000
	Service manager	3,000	3,000	3,000	3,000	3,000	3,000	3,000
	Office manager	1,600	1,600	1,600	1,600	1,600	1,600	1,600
	Receptionist	900	900	900	900	900	900	900
	Total A	16,100	17,200	17,400	21,000	22,000	22,700	27,300
B.	Advertising and promotion Advertising/mailouts, etc.	15,000	7,500	7,500	7,500	7,500	7,500	7,500
	Travel and entertainment	500	500	500	500	600	600	600
	Total B	15,500	8,000	8,000	8,000	8,100	8,100	8,100
C.	Leasing — Equipment/ furniture	2,000	2,000	2,000	2,000	2,000	2,000	2,000
D.	Rent — Building/land	7,000	7,000	7,000	7,000	7,000	7,000	7,000
E.	Supplies and Services: Supplies — Shop	600	600	600	600	600	600	800
	— Office	300	300	300	300	300	300	400
	Utilities	600	600	600	600	600	600	700
	Maintenance	400	400	400	400	400	400	400
	Telephone/yellow pages	800	800	800	800	800	800	800
	Laundry	400	400	400	400	400	400	400
	Contract title $15/Veh.	120	150	195	255	315	360	390
	Total E	3,220	3,250	3,295	3,355	3,415	3,460	3,890
F.	Professional services Accounting	300	300	300	300	300	300	300
	Legal	300	300	300	300	300	300	300
	Management	2,500	2,500	2,500	2,500	2,500	2,500	2,500
	Total F	3,100	3,100	3,100	3,100	3,100	3,100	3,100
G.	Taxes — FICA/TEC	2,010	2,280	2,460	2,860	3,000	3,110	3,690
H.	Floor plan interest: Vehicles @ 20% (8-14)	1,600	1,600	2,000	2,000	2,000	2,400	2,400
	Demos @ 23% (4)	920	920	920	920	920	920	920
	Total H	2,520	2,520	2,920	2,920	2,920	3,320	3,320
I.	Insurance	1,500	1,500	1,500	1,500	1,500	1,500	1,500
J.	Others: Memberships	250	250	250	250	250	250	250
	Subscriptions	50	50	50	50	50	50	50
	Miscellaneous (contingency)	400	400	400	400	400	400	400
	Total J	700	700	700	700	700	700	700
	TOTAL EXPENSES	53,650	47,550	48,375	52,435	53,735	54,990	60,600
	OPERATING INCOME	(30,050)	(16,750)	(8,075)	(4,935)	1,765	5,610	7,000
	Add: Leasing profit	50	100	150	250	350	450	600
	Less: Interest — bank loan	3,500	3,500	3,500	3,500	3,500	3,500	3,500
	Net profit before tax	(33,500)	(20,150)	(11,425)	(8,185)	(1,385)	2,560	4,100
	Income tax	0	0	0	0	0	0	0
	Net profit after tax	(33,500)	(20,150)	(11,425)	(8,185)	(1,385)	2,560	4,100

[a]Includes total tax payment for the first year's operations

[b]Interest payments are for residual long term debt of $150,000 in the 2nd year and $50,000 in the 3rd year @ 21%

	April	May	June	July	1982 Aug.	1st Year Total 12 months	2nd Year Sept. 82 to Aug. 83	3rd Year Sept. 83 to Aug. 84
	238,000	252,000	280,000	308,000	350,000	2,296,000	5,040,000	5,880,000
	17	18	20	22	25	164	360	420
	70,000	70,000	80,000	80,000	90,000	675,000	1,320,000	1,600,000
	14	14	16	16	18	135	264	320
	28,000	33,000	35,000	38,000	40,000	300,000	720,000	840,000
	12,000	12,000	12,000	14,000	15,000	117,000	216,000	250,000
	16,000	19,000	20,000	21,000	22,000	178,000	432,000	504,000
	364,000	386,000	427,000	461,000	517,000	3,566,000	7,728,000	9,074,000
	35,700	37,800	42,000	46,200	52,500	344,400	720,000	756,000
	12,600	12,600	14,400	14,400	16,200	121,500	237,600	288,000
	16,800	19,800	21,000	22,800	24,000	180,000	432,000	504,000
	4,800	4,800	4,800	5,600	6,000	46,800	86,400	100,000
	9,600	11,400	12,000	12,600	13,200	106,800	259,200	302,400
	79,500	86,400	94,200	101,600	111,900	799,500	1,735,200	1,950,400
	8,900	9,400	10,500	11,500	13,100	85,700	180,000	189,000
	3,100	3,100	3,600	3,600	4,000	30,200	59,400	72,000
	1,300	1,800	1,000	0	1,500	17,200	18,000	20,000
	1,600	1,600	1,600	1,600	1,600	19,200	28,800	28,800
	2,300	2,300	2,300	2,300	2,300	22,800	42,000	46,000
	5,000	5,000	5,000	5,000	5,000	51,000	72,000	78,000
							30,000	36,000
	3,000	3,000	3,000	3,000	3,000	36,000	48,000	54,000
	1,600	1,600	1,600	1,600	1,600	19,200	21,600	24,000
	900	900	900	900	900	10,800	12,000	13,200
	27,700	28,700	29,500	29,500	33,000	292,100	511,800	561,000
	7,500	7,500	7,500	7,500	7,500	97,500	102,000	114,000
	600	600	600	600	600	6,800	10,800	12,000
	8,100	8,100	8,100	8,100	8,100	104,300	112,800	126,000
	2,000	3,000	3,000	3,000	3,000	28,000	42,000	42,000
	7,000	7,000	7,000	7,000	7,000	84,000	96,000	96,000
	800	800	800	800	800	8,400	12,000	12,000
	400	400	400	400	400	4,200	7,200	7,200
	700	700	700	700	700	7,800	10,800	12,000
	400	400	400	400	400	4,800	6,000	6,000
	800	800	800	800	800	9,600	11,000	11,000
	400	400	400	400	400	4,800	6,000	6,000
	465	480	540	570	645	4,485	9,360	11,100
	3,965	3,980	4,040	4,070	4,145	44,085	62,360	65,300
	300	300	300	300	300	3,600	4,000	4,000
	300	300	300	300	300	3,600	4,200	4,200
	2,500	2,500	2,500	2,500	2,500	30,000	36,000	36,000
	3,100	3,100	3,100	3,100	3,100	37,200	44,200	44,200
	3,390	3,740	3,550	3,620	4,100	37,810	88,380	99,300
	2,400	2,400	2,800	2,800	2,800	27,200	48,000	57,600
	920	920	920	920	920	11,040	11,040	11,040
	3,320	3,320	3,720	3,720	3,720	38,240	59,040	68,640
	1,500	1,500	1,500	1,500	1,500	18,000	24,000	24,000
	250	250	250	250	250	3,000	3,600	4,000
	50	50	50	50	50	600	800	800
	400	400	400	400	400	4,800	7,200	9,600
	700	700	700	700	700	8,400	11,600	14,400
	60,775	63,140	64,210	64,310	68,365	692,135	1,052,180	1,140,840
	18,725	23,260	29,990	37,290	43,535	107,365	683,020	809,560
	750	950	1,150	1,350	1,600	7,750	27,000	36,000
	3,500	3,500	3,500	3,500	3,500	42,000	31,500[b]	10,500[b]
	15,975	20,710	27,640	35,140	41,635	73,115	678,520	835,060
	0	0	0	0	20,796[a]	20,796	292,869	362,750
	15,975	20,710	27,640	35,140	20,839	52,319	385,651	472,310

	2nd Yr.	3rd Yr.
Profit Before Tax	8.8% of Sales,	9.2% of Sales
Profit After Tax	5.0% of Sales,	5.2% of Sales

Electric Cars of Houston
Cash Forecast
For the Period September, 1981 Thru August, 1984 (3 Years)

	1981 Sept.	Oct.	Nov.	Dec.	1982 Jan.	Feb.
Cash Balance — Starting Equity of $35,000	35,000	106,500	86,350	74,925	66,740	65,335
Add: Cash Receipts						
Gross Profit: New Vehicles, Used Vehicles, Service, Tires and Parts	23,600	30,800	40,300	47,500	55,500	60,600
Leasing Profit	50	100	150	250	350	450
Long-Term Debt	200,000					
Total Cash Available	258,650	137,400	126,800	122,675	122,590	126,405
Less: Cash Disbursements						
Salaries/Commissions	16,100	17,200	17,400	21,000	22,000	22,700
Advertising and Promotion	15,500	8,000	8,000	8,000	8,100	8,100
Leasing-Equipment/ Furniture	2,000	2,000	2,000	2,000	2,000	2,000
Rent-Building/Land	7,000	7,000	7,000	7,000	7,000	7,000
Supplies and Services	3,220	3,250	3,295	3,355	3,415	3,460
Professional Services	3,100	3,100	3,100	3,100	3,100	3,100
Taxes-FICA/TEC	2,010	2,280	2,460	2,860	3,000	3,110
Floor Plan-Interest	2,520	2,520	2,920	2,920	2,920	3,320
Insurance	1,500	1,500	1,500	1,500	1,500	1,500
Memberships, Subscriptions and Misc.	700	700	700	700	700	700
Federal Income Tax						
Inventory						
Used Cars	25,000					
Parts- Electric	10,000					
Conventional	10,000					
Tires	15,000					
Renovation/Improvements	20,000					
Deposits	2,000					
Reimbursement–Start-up	13,000					
Total Disbursements	148,650	47,550	48,375	52,435	53,735	54,990
Tentative Cash Balance	110,000	89,850	78,425	70,240	68,855	71,415
Repayment of L.T. Debt						
Interest Payment on L.T. Debt (21%)	3,500	3,500	3,500	3,500	3,500	3,500
Ending Cash Balance	106,500	86,350	74,925	66,740	65,355	67,915
Loan Balance	200,000	200,000	200,000	200,000	200,000	200,000

Mar.	Apr.	May	June	July	Aug.	1st Yr. Total 12 Mo.	2nd Yr. Sept. '82 to Aug. '83	3rd Yr. Sept. '83 to Aug. '84
67,915	72,015	62,990	83,700	81,340	116,480	35,000	137,319	312,970
67,600	79,500	86,400	94,200	101,600	111,900	799,500	1,735,200	1,950,400
600	750	'950	1,150	1,350	1,600	7,750	27,000	36,000
						200,000		
136,115	152,265	150,340	179,050	184,290	229,980	1,042,250	1,899,519	1,199,270
27,300	27,700	28,700	29,500	29,500	33,000	292,100	511,800	561,000
8,100	8,100	8,100	8,100	8,100	8,100	104,300	112,800	126,000
2,000	2,000	3,000	3,000	3,000	3,000	28,000	42,000	42,000
7,000	7,000	7,000	7,000	7,000	7,000	84,000	96,000	96,000
3,890	3,965	3,980	4,040	4,070	4,145	44,085	62,360	65,300
3,100	3,100	3,100	3,100	3,100	3,100	37,200	44,200	44,200
3,690	3,390	3,740	3,550	3,620	4,100	37,810	88,380	99,300
3,320	3,320	3,320	3,720	3,720	3,720	38,240	59,040	68,640
1,500	1,500	1,500	1,500	1,500	1,500	18,000	24,000	24,000
700	700	700	700	700	700	8,400	11,600	14,400
					20,796	20,796	292,869	362,750
	10,000		10,000			45,000	50,000	40,000
	4,000					14,000	20,000	5,000
	8,000		15,000			33,000	50,000	25,000
	3,000		5,000			23,000	10,000	10,000
						20,000	30,000	0
						2,000	0	0
						13,000	0	0
60,600	85,775	63,140	94,210	64,310	89,161	862,931	1,505,049	1,583,590
75,515	66,490	87,200	84,840	119,980	140,819	179,319	394,470	715,780
						0	50,000	100,000
3,500	3,500	3,500	3,500	3,500	3,500	42,000	31,500	10,500
72,015	62,990	83,700	81,340	116,480	137,319	137,319	312,970	605,280
200,000	200,000	200,000	200,000	200,000	200,000	200,000	150,000	50,000

Index